WING IT

6 Simple Steps to Succeed as a
Modern Day Parent

Anastasia Gavalas, MS, SDA

WING IT

ALSO BY ANASTASIA GAVALAS

Leadership Through the Eyes of Children

THIS BOOK IS DEDICATED TO

Gabriella, Chloe, Artemi, Harrison, & Jeorgiana

My greatest teachers throughout this amazing
parenthood journey
XOXOX

CONTENTS

Introduction

DOES IT EVER GET EASIER?

*Parenting is not about what you do with your child,
It is about who you are to your child. - Gordon Neufeld*

This book cannot be timelier. The current culture of the world exhibits consequences of disengaged philosophies and imbalanced practices both in parenting and education. The urgency to restore harmony to this chaotic circumstance has reached a climax and it is vital that parents get a grasp and establish a new normal in this existing muddled state of parenting. The *Wing It* formula brings real clarity and confidence to the national discussion by realizing parents' strongest affect is when they fully accept themselves and the lessons children are here to teach them. Of all the varieties of parenting practices that stem from fear, there desperately needs to be a return to beliefs that encourage cooperation and opportunities for children and parents to flourish together easily.

Unlike other parenting books, *Wing It* introduces an approach that is achievable by everyone. Insight shared in this book will surely cause a different kind of awakening for parents. It ends the meaningless overload of past ominous practices that squander people's chances to live joyfully and welcome new paradigms in parenting that value personal awareness and cultivate empowerment. It helps children's individual personalities to emerge while being guided appropriately by parents who strive for happiness and fulfillment. *Wing It* will launch readers to discover uncomplicated parenting styles by respecting individual strengths and ceasing the use of ineffective techniques. It provides parents with ideas on how to plug-in, build valiant foundations with authentic principles, and use personal intuition to make sweeping connections that help families thrive. Respectfully, it will enlighten parents to return to good judgment and wisdom by honoring diverse perspectives and the varied definitions of success.

There is much more to raising children today than scare tactics, heartless data, and combative philosophies that can bring out the best in this rapidly developing generation. In this two-part guidebook for raising children, readers can design a lifestyle that is perfect for them and their families. Part I: *Root It*, consists of five chapters that take the pressure off of perfection and root families in stability as they erect strong foundations and new ways of thinking. Part II: *Wing It* provides parents the practical teachings and strategies that build balance and responsiveness as they conscientiously choose to raise independent thinkers and children that strive for fulfillment.

Revealing illustrations will help distinguish patterns that can be beneficial to parents as they grow their own families. And contemporary perspectives will help elevate parenting to a new level of success for anyone who is willing to trust in the process. *Wing It* provides readers with the means to form essential foundations for new beliefs and innovative designs for living in today's world.

Readers of this book are progressive, intelligent, forward-thinking caregivers who are tired of fear-based parenting approaches that control children rather than liberate. Their consciousness continually reminds them of the impact their own wellness and fulfillment has on raising self-reliant, independent, caring children. They understand that encouraging children to be independent thinkers profoundly empowers them. Fundamentally, parents will self-reflect, develop confidence, and redefine success in parenting as they form new belief systems individualized to their families. The *Wing It* way facilitates intuitive wisdom and organic life progress while actively engaging parents in the art of parenting with ease in modern day life.

The fundamental thinking in this book presents 21st century parenting as a sensible, re-harmonizing, proactive, freeing journey to new perspectives and customized skill sets for parents wishing to improve their lives naturally. This is a revolutionary new concept in the parenting landscape of today, and a style that is incredibly relevant to parents from all walks of life, at all stages of development, across our nation, as well as all over the world. The *Wing It* way of thinking will resonate with anyone who is ready to move forward and raise children with the absence of limiting beliefs and fear-based approaches. Parents today are ready to break free from current maddening reactions that drive an ever-increasing force of counterintuitive parenting approaches and exhaust parents' time, energy, and resources.

Today, most parents are tired of being tired and want relief from this overload of anxiety-ridden traditions. But, before parents can take on the greatest challenge of raising children, they need to recognize unnecessary patterns and an emerging sense of purpose. The *Wing It* formula teaches how to best reach personal satisfaction while realistically providing children with the roots and wings essential for success in today's complex world. It presents tools that help parents honor how each child is different and stay attuned to what makes them unique. With this cooperative approach readers will be led to a discovery of loving principles and supportive practices that launch children to their individual potential.

Wing It builds essential bridges of opportunity that unite the simplicity of the past with the resolve to take readers further emotionally, intellectually, spiritually, and physically in today's modern world. It links the thought-provoking present day challenges with solutions that encourage readers to get back into the driver's seat to parent as this generation must, with confidence and ease. Times like these, when values have been warped by fear-based ideas, call for independent thinking and innovative planning. This book will help readers birth deep commitments to personal values and acceptance that brings forth the best in humanity and create culturally responsive families. Simple awareness and implementation of the *Wing It* ideas gives people the courage to connect authentically and succeed with satisfaction. It's an approach of another kind for parents who want to relax their grip in a complex world that deserves simplicity.

Readers can discover inclusive belief systems and simplistic parenting approaches that celebrate diversity and launch independence for journeys like no other. It is my hope that this book will serve as a guide to help parents further their evolution by honoring the amazing people they are and help them develop a vision for parenting that fosters true acceptance and unconditional love. Those committed to these ideas can marinate in the deliciousness of raising children; from the warm cuddles to the maddening defiance, from the milestones of firsts to the brilliantly elaborate exchanges as they grow. Infinite bonds of love will develop and flourish making the process magnificent for both parent and child.

Wing It was born out of love and confidence in the human possibility. It relies on the bona fide belief that everyone has the power within to live a joyous life with children. There is no longer a need to feel pressured or fall into societal traps of labeling children, their development, or judge actions. The philosophy presented in this book has been cultivated through my work with children, parents, teachers, and caregivers for over 20 years. What I know for sure is that each family is so beautifully diverse and each person within that family has the potential to reach success. Those who have belief systems and principles that respect and support their strengths will have an easier time reaching a fulfilling life. *Wing It* provides successful strategies that support the individual construction of a foundation that can make life happier, goals achievable, and dreams a reality.

Dynamics in relationships will change for the better as readers infuse these soulful, yet practical, principles into their real-life, day-to-day living.

This book celebrates diversity of perspectives for all kinds of individuals and families, by focusing on the power of mind, body, and spirit connections. It honors the importance of grounding humanity in love while encouraging the extension of wings so that individuals realize their potential. It guides readers out of fear-based parenting actions, language, and beliefs and into more present, nurturing, joyful, innate, freeing, and respectful journeys with children. It details the organic steps parents need to take to end struggles and build connections, to fulfill themselves with the purpose of becoming the best human beings for their children. *Wing It* reminds us to simply live mindfully, honor the purpose of our lives, and the spirits of all children.

Being a parent is an amazing opportunity to reflect on life and stay connected to all that is wondrous in life. Individuals who build their own courageous presence with the parenting ideals that are right for them, free themselves from pressure, insecurity, worry, and resistance. They uncover their authentic, brilliant, powerful selves and experience joy in parenthood. A solid parenting philosophy will strengthen the resolve to seek approval and helps individuals become who they aspire to be by acquiring a plan that makes sense and expands their influence in a loving way. What a magnificent gift becoming a parent presents to humanity. This moment allows people to rise above the distortion of the mass push for consent and appreciate individual journeys as people live within their naturally uncomplicated circumstances.

The *Wing It* theory promotes a balance of grounding and freeing opportunities for readers to interact comfortably with the modern world. It deters parents from going to extremes in order for children to succeed and helps their expectations unite with the well being and aspirations of their children. Individuals who feel supported as dynamic life contributors are more likely to raise children in a safe, engaging, and productive way. Releasing people from the obsessive need to be perfect or mimic collective ideas from superfluous parenting trends will also liberate children to be their best.

People who take themselves too seriously make life harder than it has to be. Using fear-based approaches with children creates a limiting cyclical pattern that stunts individual potential. Children are not to be controlled, but guided and life is not meant to be hard but, to enjoy.

People who are able to release their grip on perfection dynamically create spaces to enjoy life more and begin moving forward with ease. There is no one-size-fits-all solution for parents who want to be successful in today's world. However, the formula presented in this book integrates elements that naturally lead people to live happier and more fulfilling lives with children. *Wing It* improves people's ability to create new paradigms in parenting that work brilliantly for them and their families, at their own pace, and on their own terms.

Part One

ROOT IT

Chapter 1

A BATTLE TO PERFECTION

There are two basic motivating forces: fear and love. When we are afraid, we pull back from life. When we are in love, we open to all that life has to offer with passion, excitement, and acceptance. We need to learn to love ourselves first, in all our glory and our imperfections. If we cannot love ourselves, we cannot fully open to our ability to love others or our potential to create. Evolution and all hopes for a better world rest in the fearlessness and open-hearted vision of people who embrace life.
- John Lennon -

This has truly been a period of revolutions and chaos. No more has it been felt then in the lives of those who are trying to raise children during these complex times. The disturbing echoes of uprisings, disasters, rampages, protests, abuse, and attacks naturally seep into each and every home regardless of defensive actions taken.

Parents, nowadays, try fiercely to make sense of the intense responsibilities, overbearing sights and sounds of global turmoil, national debates, personal obstacles, reality television, and what they personally experienced being raised during a very different era in parenting. One can easily quote Dickens, "These are the best of times, these are the worst of times."

Today, like never before, there exists a generation that has been allowed the opportunity to examine the effects their own parents had on their lives. Modern day people who have access to an unprecedented amount of information and often disparaging reflections that help them decipher personal inadequacies or unhappiness resulting from their childhoods.

For most, this primary recognition barely leads them to learn how to take their lives back and, even more frightening, will be the prime incentive for future dysfunctional practices. Regardless of any personal wounds, beliefs, or cultural experiences, this new generation overwhelmingly agrees on one definitive impetus - they want to be better parents.

In wild attempts to compensate for the bad parenting done to most of them, people have birthed circumstances that encompass fear-based mindsets, immense imbalance of power, vast unhealthy behaviors, and extreme parenting approaches. The struggle in how to stay safe in an unpredictable world and raise children successfully has become the newest crusade of the 21st century. The potency lies in the ferocity from individuals who, while behind closed doors battle with their own insecurities, also remain in an intense quest to produce their variety of the perfect child.

Approaches to parenting at this time generally represent two distinct mind-sets: an extraordinary resurgence of fear-based beliefs and an intense rebuttal against individual childhoods. This has birthed failing parenting practices that promote hovering and exaggeratedly inconsistent behaviors.

There are parents who imitate their own dysfunctional upbringings because they have yet to disentangle painful encumbrances, while others take on models that amplify the opposite of how they were raised under the pretext of knowing better. More often than not, today's parents utilize their own children as personal projects to be perfected or as individual remedies to feel better about themselves.

These examples can be found across every country and ethnic group, in wealthy communities and poor, and in every religion and lifestyle. These practices do not distinguish people by their cast, class, or tradition. But rather, encompass the totality of the modern day parenting arena with fears, confusion, and ongoing failures.

Even though the evolution of families has been steadily emerging, the way people approach parenting has retreated to a very unenlightened, reactive, coarse manner. We can easily find parenting trends, even from the last century, that are irrelevant and completely unsuitable for today's progressive, global world.

It has become more like a *Battle to Perfection* of unfit approaches for parents whose expectations are constantly being ramped up to extremes. As a result, today's generation has lost their sensibility and confidence and children have gained stress-based ailments, new addictions, and destructive behaviors. Parents have allowed society to eradicate intuitive wisdom in their efforts of how-to raise healthy, smart, well-rounded, successful children.

With primordial fears affixed to every move in child-rearing and exploitative parenting examples highlighted in the media, there arises an uncertainty among even the most intelligent adults. In the past, parents gave children what they "needed" whereas today's adults, while stumbling at best, audaciously try to give into children's "wants." This has resulted in a whole new set of confused approaches in the parenting arena.

As the entire planet experiences great instability, unforeseeable challenges, periods of major shifts and leading change, so has the landscape of parenting. People, like never before, are imbued with elevated levels of alert that often have no bearing on them personally, yet fundamentally affect the way they live and raise children. Present day parents have greater chances of harming their children by practicing extreme parenting approaches than worrying about the potential extremists risks that saturate American society.

Two really prominent excessive practices that exist today are over-parenting and over-permissiveness. These ideas have initiated a fundamental collapse in the reasonable actions parents need to sustain when raising today's children. Families, across the map, are tanking due to inconsistent approaches used under the guise of safeguarding children.

The recent menagerie of flawed techniques, whether tigerish or hovering, neglectful or over-indulgent, controlling or competitive, and influenced by different cultures around the world often lack the incredible need for personal insight.

Today, life for children is inundated with all types of alarming influences, defense mechanisms, safety devices, shocking stories, recalls, predators, bullying, over-testing, vaccines, immunizations, baby-proofing, stranger danger, cyber bullying, and tons of crises around the globe which collectively hinder parents from creating the life they desire.

Parallel to that is the excessive number of children being diagnosed with food intolerances, chronic ailments, additional hypersensitivities, and mental disorders regardless of the substantial boost in parental efforts to continually stay ahead of protecting their young by not letting them go more than fifteen minutes without a dose of Purell. These new uncertainties, deep concerns, and an accelerated alignment with fear have caused exhaustion and distress, leading parents in a fervent search to try something that is reliable and successful for raising today's children.

Parenting to perfection is all just an illusion. Individuals who strive for that often miss the opportunities that fortify individual greatness. Some people adopt their own parents' values while others completely reject their parents' approaches to how they were raised as children. In an effort to grasp the varying ephemeral "good parent stamp of approval" people frequently tally opinions of others. Social acceptance is sometimes more valued than personal accord. The real prizes and approbations *Wing It* parenting promotes are the moment-to-moment periods of enlightenment and simple consideration of love throughout personal journeys that are genuine and enrich life experiences.

Needing to attain the approval of others, trying to prove one's worth in exchange for love, or anticipating recognition for "perfection" in parenting only delays self-evolution. The actual rewards are in the "knowing" you did your absolute best and are striving for a fulfilling life. Letting go of external expectations of what should be happening at every moment in life allows one to create a life that is personally true for them. Anything and everything is possible. Today, human beings live in the most diverse of times where value and acceptance can bring forth the best in humanity. The path to fulfillment wisely integrates organic, timeless virtues with forward-thinking global perspectives to help circumscribe significant experiences.

Courage. That is what launches an awakening in parenting. It takes courage to be reflective and satisfied with experiences in parenthood. How one defines successful parenting is up to each individual. Grasping after perfection or external approval wastes time and robs humans of personal empowerment and joy. Acknowledging and valuing specific journeys helps rid the need for seeking outside approval thus creating the environment and experiences that are right for each individual family.

Whether someone's childhood was full of joy or despair, the approach in parenting, must consist of a conscious acknowledgement, articulation, and acceptance of the past in order to move forward and become a better parent. Supportive, encouraging upbringings as well as painful, embarrassing criticism from adults shape the course of a child's future.

Within either scenario, the manner in which someone is raised can cause future worthiness issues and self-doubt, and for others it can strengthen their resolve to be different in their ways.

Childhood experiences determine the level of self-acceptance, need for approval, and individual expectations, that are emphasized primarily when they themselves become parents. Innovative ideas offered in *Wing It* help release judgment and pressures while guiding parents toward a style that is right for them. All forward progress begins with truly letting go and a discovery of one's potential.

As a young girl, despite a mouth full of braces and an awful bi-level haircut that was never meant for curly hair, I believed in possibilities and an optimistic life. I found my upbringing to be strict at times but, nonetheless similar to other first generation European-American children. Strong criticisms prevailed. The insistence that there was only one right answer was generally from the oldest male in the house. I observed, endured, and swore I would parent differently. Ironically, I still hoped for a good parenting stamp of approval when I became a parent, even from those whose parenting I didn't agree with.

I was brought up to believe certain things that were passed down from generation to generation. Some of those thought forms were loving while others were shaped by fear. The insight into the factors leading me to writing this book strengthened my conclusion that parents nowadays can certainly experience parenthood differently regardless of past practices and experiences. And today, more than ever, they can do it with greater ease and more success.

What brings you here? Whether it is preemptive worry or progressive open-mindedness, your only responsibility and ability as a parent is to awaken to the possibilities within you. People generally spend valuable time planning and predicting what is yet to come. Head chatter burdens them with lots of ifs and buts, hesitations and hurriedness that preclude real life living. Times that present challenges and are set in anguish are not always appreciated for being powerful moments of expansion.

Today's parents have the challenge of balancing interpersonal skills with intrapersonal skills. It is the balance between the skills of a good salesperson and the ability to have an accurate view of one self. Regardless of whether or not one disregards or accepts the way they were raised, and despite embracing pre-conceived rules written by society, no one is vaccinated against adversity in parenting. Each person has to do the work and be realistic and productive with the work they do. There can be a balance of holding high expectations and remaining loving to build a happy life for you and your family.

An over-arching means toward leading a fulfilled life means a different way of thinking, one that blends wisdom with a focus on expansion, absent of any *Battle to Perfection*. Striving for wholeness with high expectations is possible and can be done tenderly. Putting efforts into perfection often leads to disappointment.

Now is a good time for parents to reach for uncomplicated experiences and to accept the interconnectedness of mind, body, and soul. It is a new way of thinking in this fast moving era defined by its radical progress and diversity. Parents nowadays need the strength, vision, and grace to be themselves and find their ideal life. They need new strategies, like those presented in this book, in order to liberate responses and rethink everything they ever imagined parenthood could be.

A Battle to Perfection is instigated from one simple thought, the fear of failure. Every single person has a choice to live in fear or not. Reaching a higher realm is all about becoming fearless, being true to one self, and living from the heart. This naturally releases any urge to compete or compare. Individuals who magnetize confident love have no room in their lives to allow fear to intimidate them. In all opportunities, it is the will to change and capacity to listen to one's heart that determines the outcome. Every dysfunction in life and in parenting comes from fear.

Knowing how to tackle worry promotes harmony, alignment, and empowerment. This remains challenging being that we live in a fear-based society. However, knowing that once fear decreases, performance increases can lead people to an open-minded place that brings about loving parenting.

Climates that foster fear-based beliefs create apprehension and doubt. Things that are feared are automatically given power. Practicing fear-elimination in simple ways allows people to move towards harmony, flexibility, and empowerment. This intentional act of living freely is a choice. It embraces finding appreciation in any way possible, not allowing joys to be squandered by anxiety, preserving joyous moments, and celebrating open-minded advancements one step at a time.

Surrendering the goal of trying to please everyone allows people to start taking care of themselves and welcome love, joy, and independence in their day-to-day practices. Also, learning to say no to things that are uncooperative, drowning, alarming, and negative that appear in one's environment helps people shield themselves from fear-based living. It's better to have a few people and things in your life that represent love, than a life jam-packed with things that hinder happiness. Less is more.

How do people eliminate fear, especially at a time when parents are bombarded with "experts" and "professionals" about test performance or potential risks that may arise? Understanding that fear is learned and, can be unlearned. It's about exercising the muscle of confidence. Fear's limiting impression often leads to crippling anxiety, worry, distortion, and even depression. Physical results are often the causes of stress and fear built up in the body. Fear-elimination takes emotional courage and physical action.

Being victorious despite any battles involves choosing faith and confidence while leaning away from apprehensions. The further you get, the clearer you will be about how you can reach peace and happiness with your family. Each person has that ability and can shift, moment-by-moment and choice-by-choice. Today's parents are naturally brave. They are courageous in their willingness to engage and courageous in their ability to implement new ideas to move forward.

Personal thoughts and stories influence happiness. Start telling yourself a new story because the stories people tell themselves can either empower them or stifle growth. Today's parents need to live bravely with optimism and hope for this amazingly unique generation of children they are raising. Those who believe in their unlimited possibilities and trust their inner wisdom gain strength in their convictions and lead less fearful lives. Create thoughts and stories that encourage confidence and boost mind-sets.

The first shift is to be mindful whenever there is an awareness of an unsettling thought. Staying alert of where there is trepidation and taking small but continuous steps to identify feelings and bring awareness organically brings change. This can help assess concerns and personal truth while creating a push toward empowerment. This way, people can fluently act on their own truth by staying in the perfect path for what they desire.

If you want a calmer, safer, lifestyle of freedom then simply believe it is possible. Take advantage of those experiences that support that way of thinking by remaining curious not fearful and utilize mistakes and challenges as opportunities to expand and grow. Designing a life that is fitting for each individual involves finding independent solutions, building courage, and dissolving fears. Making this connection shifts people from living fearfully to fearlessly living. True freedom is living fearlessly.

The drive for perfection becomes exaggerated when people take on the role of parenting. Out of fear, parents are dismissing their own innate wisdom and wind up surrendering to unhealthy expectations that cause stress and unhappiness. What the outside world dictates about what parents "should do" or "should be" is impractical and hinders progress.

Parenting doesn't have to be a fight or competition of any sort, or as hard as it is for that matter. It becomes hard when individuals make it hard. Those who align themselves with superfluous ideas plunge in their own *Battle to Perfection* when trying to attain things that are irrelevant and unnatural for them personally. And parents who choose disingenuous approaches or goals that do not correlate with their innate knowing make it harder than it is.

There needs to be a major halt in the way individuals attempt to live up to the illusions of perfection and success by other people's definitions. All too often, people have lost the capacity to live joyfully because they are chasing after someone else's concept of the perfect life and measuring themselves by what they lack. The moment a person becomes open to individual possibility they create a welcoming space for them to design their perfect life.

In this new paradigm- the *Wing It* way, parents who retract from external notions of what perfection is and, are able to find the "perfect" in their own ideas and families boldly create successful formulas that work for their individual lives. The amazing part of life is that there exists gazillions of possibilities that can lead parents to happy and successful lives, and paths that are much easier and more fulfilling.

It's simply a matter of becoming thoroughly authentic, giving life your highest intention, and believing in a greater purpose. Internalizing the ideas presented in this book helps take the pressure off parents by welcoming a uniquely simple and more realistic approach to follow in order to find each parent's "perfect."

Individuals define perfection for themselves. The "perfect" life is something each person shapes with his or her choices. And each choice empowers people, which leads them towards greater understanding. The trajectory of someone's life is determined by how open they are to making choices that shift them towards feeling fulfilled with the life experiences they create. In this case, the intentions behind those choices influence the experience of a family.

Chapter 2

DID YOUR PARENTS SCREW YOU UP?

To accomplish great things, we must not only act,
but also dream, not only plan, but also believe.
- Anatole France -

Knowing who you are in life is essential. A willingness to participate in an uncompromising journey of reflection, faith, and progressive thinking will guide you through life. "What kind of life do you want?" Sit with those thoughts for a while as your inner voice sifts through the more complex emotions.

Your belief system is the motivation behind the "how" and "why" you live the way you do. It is your personal image of truth. Think about your relationship to this very moment as you sit with this book in hand. What brought you to this moment? What do you need in your life today to be happier? What do you need in your overall wellness to feel fantastic? What do you need in your life, your relationships, and your parenting to reach fulfillment?

Belief systems are the foundation which parenting approaches are developed. They are the thought forms that develop as we grow from childhood on. The key to choosing exactly what one desires in life is in the mindful construction of a purposeful approach, a well-balanced system. The moment someone becomes a parent there needs to be a climactic overthrow of any past unconstructive mistruths within their belief systems if they wish to parent well.

This exercise may feel frightening or manipulative at first. But, challenging the integrity of one's own convictions with knowledge, faith, and openness allows for greater confidence and more accurate perceptions. People who remain open and avoid judging that which they don't understand receive fresh new views of themselves and their parenting. Those who are able to reflect on their past and discover benefits, recognize the significance in life as a whole journey and are ready to help others discover their valuable presence.

Did Your Parents Screw You Up? From relationship issues to cancer, everyone can find something to blame on their parents. Past generations have been conditioned to be judgmental about their development and want to change how they parent. Our backgrounds and circumstances undoubtedly influence who we are, but we are ultimately responsible for who we become and how we parent.

By shifting perspectives people can ease sharp distinctions from the past and find a space that feels right for today's challenges. Life experiences are not permanent and when parents accept their past and begin to move forward in an optimistic way they can begin to live life with greater ease and less pressure. Once people acquire this awareness, confidence grows and people are able create a life by design that is directed by uplifting thoughts and revels in individual uniqueness.

This new way of thinking, which is taking the responsibility of becoming a co-creator of life, will allow for brilliant partnerships of mind, body, and soul. People who have great lives possess belief systems set in high expectations. Their parents may have screwed things up for them one way or another, or many times for that matter. However, they have developed a deep sense of worth and believe in personal responsibility so as to willfully construct prosperous lives. Those who deliberately bridge life opportunities lovingly with high-quality choices move toward genuine fulfillment.

They generate actions that are pleasing to them. These individuals set themselves up for success by owning a solid sense of self worth that supports optimistic belief systems within their lives, allowing them to continually sow seeds of happiness, gaining momentum as they continue walking in their truth. Everyone has the potential to grow new belief systems that create solid, contemporary standards, and support their evolution, no matter their past.

The world inundates people with great hindrances that cause unconstructive belief systems and the stories attached to them to impede progress. These systems shape lives negatively by inhibiting a person's best character traits. A shift in the makeup of these thought forms is possible when people become aware of the obstruction they cause. Modification in what and who people surround themselves with, along with consciously planning what they aspire, removes emotional layers that impede social, emotional, cognitive, or physical progress.

There are many paths a person can take in pursuit of rediscovering greatness within and begin to live a more constructive life, once they gain the clarity and conviction of what they believe to be true in their heart. This is determined by that which is thought and subsequently embedded in personal belief systems.

Each person's individual growth increases by how much they value themselves. Successful people deliberately create corresponding systems of belief; ideals that are in direct correlation with their authentic selves as they evolve. A person's best is infinite when their sense of worth increases in appreciation of their whole self. Becoming a parent can be a catalyst for individuals to build strong belief systems that will guide them through parenthood and life.

My belief system developed through what I observed as a child and heard from people who surrounded me, mainly my parents, grandmother, siblings, cousins, and family friends. There was little diversity in race, religion, or traditions of people within my environment. As a whole, people around me often shared explicit, pessimistic reactions or disapproval whenever there was a lack of conformity within the group. Appreciation of global views and individuality was not necessarily revered. There was a clear message of distinction between "us" and "them"; us, being proud, hard-working Greeks and them, referring to the rest of the human race.

These narrow-minded attitudes made the world feel intimidating to me as a child. Nonetheless, my inner core fiercely rejected biased perspectives. I sensed I was different early on mainly because of my physical appearance and also because of my consistently hopeful way of thinking about humanity and life. Hence, my early sense of self and belief systems were strictly molded by other people's opinions and experiences I had. Ironically enough, I grew up and became a teacher to speakers of other languages from across the globe and created a multicultural education program for all children that focused on building an appreciation for diversity.

Parents' personal burdens mask their true spirits and can impede a child's intuitive wisdom and progression. Children are born flawless. It's the outside world that causes encumbrances, which mask their perfection. Insensitive actions, wounding words, and biased perspectives have an enormous impact on a child's belief systems. That is why parents who are aware of their personal viewpoints and reflect, as they are growing new belief systems, have an easier time in navigating their child's ideology.

Parents who are disconnected from their sense of self worth exhibit considerably different outlooks than those who have an elevated sense of who they are and what they believe in. Parents who wisely practice unconditional love and acceptance with their children cultivate rich foundations as they teach by example and strongly influence their children's belief systems.

Anyone can change by gaining new perspectives and beliefs that align with an optimistic vision. Parents stand at the doorway to evolution as citizens and, more than ever, leaders for this new generation of spirit-conscious children. Successful parenting includes a personal approach and excludes societal rules that negate the value of individualism.

Meaningful living today consists of incremental movements toward forming responsible, contemporary values. The *Wing It* philosophy helps parents find their truth and grasp onto ideas that cultivate suitable and personal responses to the challenges of parenting in today's world.

Since becoming a mother, I have evolved from a type-A, highly structured, ambitious, routine-driven, in-the-know, read every-book-ever-written parent to a more relaxed, accepting, laugh-out-loud person who strives to experience joy in the midst of the glorious chaos that often surrounds me. I laugh everyday. I learn everyday. I change everyday. I love being a mother but undoubtedly understand the importance of honoring the woman in me as the primary step for my soul's fulfillment.

I certainly did not begin my journey with such conviction. A profound quest to find out who I was as a person, as a mother, and as a woman with purpose was necessary for my evolution. I reflected on the stories which shaped my childhood and how I identified my personal account of life experiences along with getting clear about what it was that I needed to reach fulfillment.

Belief systems shape people's lives that command their actions and behaviors. When the thought forms change, so do the outcomes. Grasping on to the fact that your parents screwed you up without being able to flip it to a reflective thought about your personal progress simply wastes energy. Individuals are able to make a difference in creating more harmonious futures with the principles and beliefs they know to be right for them the moment they catch a glimpse of their potential.

Parents especially, need a clear picture of their expectations without the burdens of the past obstructing their happiness. People all too often disregard the magnitude of taking time to adapt personal belief systems with the purpose of manifesting desires. They often seem to leave the most important things in life to chance. I learned to be more conscious as I got older by examining what it was that I truly believed in and how that influenced my decisions in life.

Right before I planned on getting pregnant I began to seriously reflect on my belief systems. It was one of the most important life decisions I was going to make so I wanted to get a handle on what I expected from myself and be honest with what I believed. I had a defining moment that transformed my thinking when I was about eight months pregnant with my first child.

There was a lady in the grocery store who unknowingly made an enormous impact that shifted my parenting belief system. I had longed for clarity in defining an approach for my upcoming role, knowing I would parent differently than how I was raised. I just wasn't exactly sure of what that was going to look like. I wanted so desperately to alter any unconstructive practices and consciously shape the best environment for my children.

As I stood in the checkout line, being my tired pregnant self, my attention was often scattered. Out of the corner of my eye, I saw a beautifully elegant, tall, slim woman with long brown wavy hair that was held back by a loose low ponytail. She had Snow-White-like skin and stood in the checkout line next to mine holding a few items in her arms. She gazed straight ahead with a peaceful, carefree expression. I felt her serene, yet strong energy and what stood out more than anything was how stunningly content she was considering that way down by her feet were two young, despondent souls.

One child was in a curled up sideways position with his one leg wiping the dirty supermarket floor while the other one tugged again and again at her long flowing skirt. Each one clung on to her while whining, crying, and carrying on. She remained unruffled, exuding grace, confidence, and coolness while unconditionally loving her children.

That mother loved her children. Despite the chaos attached to her feet, she made no excuses nor did she yell or use threats in an effort to "act" like an attentive mother in front of supermarket spectators. She maintained her status, in my mind, of an illuminated example of someone who knows how to practice the art of parenting well. No words were exchanged between us. However, her calm, loving, strong manner inspired me to be the mother that I am today, especially on those days when I seem to have high levels of mayhem surrounding me.

Anyone who wants to become a better parent or teacher can make it happen by growing new belief systems. Through engagement in a reflective discovery of opportunities parents can gain meaningful insight that expands belief systems to encompass new knowledge and practices. The journey in defining one's core beliefs initiates a stunning revelation of their present reality and future potential.

Deliberate creation of balanced belief systems creates greater self-awareness and access to beneficial practices. Inspiration can be found everywhere. Gaining personal perspectives and setting firm intentions will help parents gain a more accurate sense of self in order to move away from fear-based parenting and lean towards acceptance, appreciation, and love for themselves and their children. Once people are able to articulate what they believe they will be able to create a vision and manifest it in life.

I wrote the following "I am" poem years ago. It helped me define myself and created a springboard for helping me unlock who I was in order to begin a shift towards who I wanted to become. Did my parents "screw me up" by making my siblings and me take annual pictures during hunting season (each holding a hoof) of the dead deer dad caught? Yes, but that is also what makes us who we are.

This is one of my stories. Each day brings about a new story. Tomorrow's story will be different, once again. In order for me to have a life fulfilled I must be able to continually articulate who I was, what I believe, and discover who I want to be. Then, loyally apply my new beliefs to living authentically as who I am.

I am

I am from going home for lunch throughout elementary school (not realizing just how lucky I was not to have to eat school lunches), lamb and potatoes on holidays, freshly caught porgies in the summer and venison sausage and rabbit stew in the winter. I am from dolmades, spanakopita, and hard-boiled eggs all brought to the beach by a mother who refused to buy concession stand food. I am from large family gatherings and big meals every Sunday where everyone talks at once.

I am from playing outside with my siblings in a plastic pool filled only about ¼ of the way up with water and one bucket to be shared in the summers and, building forts of snowballs 'til our fingers got numb in the snowy New York winters. I am from a curious George doll to which I told all my secrets, hand-made embroidered pants, crochet vests and hand-me-downs from my older sister. I am from back-to-school shopping at Alexander's and TSS and annual trips to the movie theater to watch Grizzly Adams movies. I am from a wood-paneled station wagon where my twin brother and I sat facing each other in the rear jump seats and the three choices of entertainment were listening to 1010wins, Yankee games, or Greek music every time we drove somewhere. I am from The Donny & Marie Show, The Love Boat, Sonny & Cher, The Jeffersons, and The Brady Bunch. I am from racing home to watch my favorite television shows like Happy Days, Bewitched, and the Bionic Woman. I am from listening to 70s & 80s disco music on authentic vinyl played on a real record player.

I am from spending full-unscheduled days outside playing, exploring, and getting home as it got dark. I am from kickball, tag, hid-n-go-

*seek, old maid, spit, and playing pool. I am from
going to our summer home on the east end of
Long Island every Friday night only to return
when the weekend was over and hearing stories
about the fun weekends my friends had. I am
from double sleepover birthday parties and my
parents not able to comprehend why the
children were too frightened to sleep
surrounded by dad's hunting trophies hanging
on the walls. I am from watching cartoons on a
Super8 reel and fighting over the one bathroom
we had to share. I am from Saturday is the day
girls cleaned house, Sundays we went to church,
and Greek school twice a week even though we
already spoke it living with Yiayia.*

*I am from good neighbors who were always
friendly and tried to comprehend our unique
cultural traditions. I am from our crossing
guard who would hold my baby dolls for me
while I went to elementary school and was one
of the greatest teachers in my life. I am from
embroidered hand-me-down jean-like pants
and wild curly hair that was often pulled back
in a high bun and sprayed with Tame.*

*I am from playing Pac-man, Space Invaders,
and Asteroids on probably the first tv-video
systems- Atari. I am from sneaking a little bit of
makeup in junior high school to electric blue
eyeliner and high hair (with the help of Stiff-
stuff) in high school. I am from off-the-shoulder
cut-off shirts, black rubber bracelets stacked up
my arm, acid-washed jeans, leg warmers over
pants, and huge, linebacker-like shoulder pads
that emphasized the glam look of the 80s.*

*I am from a Yiayia from whom I was named
after and died at the age of 92. Another yiayia
who helped raise us and still, at her age, has the
fondest memories of her life even though she lost*

a husband, a son, and experienced war first-hand. I am from a blunt father and a loyal mother who so carefully defended his ways. I am from a twin brother who has been my partner through life, an older sister who was the prettier one, and an older brother who made us laugh so hard we'd pee our pants... still does.

I am from a loud home where life lessons included sayings like, "you better marry a Greek", "cooking and cleaning is women's work", "because I said so", "I don't give a damn what your friends do", "you got a big mouth", "wait 'til your father comes home", "I will pay for your college then you're on your own", "even though I may not show it, I am proud of you."

(Addendum as of writing this book)

I am from being an intensely focused mother who believed that if parents try hard enough they can make kids do what they want, to a open-minded, appreciative-of-what-is, intuitive mom of five who learned how to allow and trust more. I am from the wisdom of the universe to appreciating my life's journey. I am from being taught by my children that life is to be treasured and lived at an unhurried pace to believing in my potential and myself. I am from reflecting on my past and looking forward to a bright future, while thinking back and smiling as I sing... "May tomorrow be a perfect day... May you find love and laughter along the way..."

The truth is, children have different perspectives about their lives as they grow. *Did Your Parents Screw You Up?* Yes. Did they also help you evolve into the wonderful person you are today? Yes. The key is to find an appreciation for the pushes and pulls of your evolution.

Parents who remain open to possibilities and form new, adaptable mindsets without allowing guilt to drive decision-making, can initiate greater appreciation for their experiences and those of their children's. A person's self-worth is a determining factor in how life is viewed and sets the tone of which opportunities are experienced.

Staying aware of personal insight while remaining fluid and responsive can manifest impressively authentic belief systems for parents that, in return have an impact on children's remembrances of their upbringings. For parents, the task remains to take time to listen, discover, and allow a new set of ideas to surface for themselves and their children so that they have the greatest propensity of creating loving journeys and fond memories of their lives.

At every stage, people and sources from all angles shower parents with information about alarming ailments to lookout for as children grow. While some fears have merit, they still need to be approached in an objective way so as not to penetrate negatively in one's belief system. In any event, too much time is wasted on negative thoughts that scare parents into unnatural states instead of enjoying life's appropriately organic, fitting experiences.

Parenthood often starts off in a triumphant state of bliss followed by periods beset with fears that can last way after children reach adulthood. Apprehensive attitudes are set in motion by agonizing worry that something will go wrong or somehow parents will screw up. This attitude hinders happiness and people who choose to gently examine negative stances can begin to detach from this unconstructive way of thinking.

Parents who feel completely accountable for their child's success are blinded by fear and directed by apprehension. By stripping away the burden and false concept that they are the sole cause of how a child is molded, parents can live with more ease and begin to shift an unconstructive belief system of "what is a good parent" to practices that are productive and achievable.

A few years back, my son's kindergarten teacher called me about a "serious" occurrence. One that she argued had to do with the fact that my son used the boy's bathroom garbage can to pee in instead of the toilet. I panicked. Because in my previous belief system "good parents" raise good children who never pee in garbage cans.

Rapid thoughts in my head concluded that he must have some kind of disorder or neurological processing glitch. After all, why would a child pee in a garbage can if they are in the bathroom? What was wrong with him? Pure self-contrived accountability led to embarrassment that flooded my being. Stupid head chatter raced around with grossly exaggerated negative thoughts. At that moment, I felt as though I was a disgraceful parent. It took a few days to process the whole less-than-a-minute ordeal that simply occurred because he had to pee really, really badly and there was another boy taking a long time using the only bathroom stall.

Another child may have held it in and gotten a bellyache while even another might have peed in his pants. Strangely enough, the more painful or humiliating decisions are more acceptable to most people. My child made the decision, instead of hurting or humiliating himself, to pee in the garbage can. It took time for me to release the shame and dim-witted judgments playing in my head. My husband and I had a conversation or two with him that, no doubt, included a hint of guilt and some talk about serious consequences for future "vulgar" behavior. I placed a false sense of failure on myself for a decision that my child made based on his all-knowing self. Necessity was the determining factor and the right choice for him at that moment in time.

Looking back, it was so stupid. As I reflect on this incident and the countless others that have come to my attention throughout my parenthood experience, I see how stunting my belief system was. I am now proud to brand myself a true work in progress.

In the past, my belief system, like many other parents, included a certainty that little people should be well-mannered, quiet, poised, and performed on demand. It was more about what it looked like to the outside world or the "window dressing" of family life than what mattered most. It was making sure the children looked good in front of relatives by dressing them impeccably and making sure they gave kisses to aunts and uncles, even if I had to whisper hard consequences and firmly steer them toward waiting, open-armed, overbearing relatives. Cultural guilt along with misperceptions of who I thought I should be as a parent sculpted my past parenting practices and belief systems.

I was the type of parent who bought every parenting and child development book available. After all, I was a teacher and had multiple degrees in education. So, naturally I believed I could intellectually figure this whole parenting thing out. I was ambitious and did countless hours of research whenever my pediatrician shared even a minuscule utterance about a possible medical aliment.

I looked the role of a "put-together" mother and may have even sounded good when I was at mommy gatherings, which presented well from an outsider's perspective, but I was exhausted. The moment I began to parent well was after I took the time to work on myself and be honest with what I needed. The second I took that guilt-free turn into being self-focused was when parenting became easier and more authentic. I began forming new belief systems and believed in myself so my day-to-day living felt less complicated and more on par for my family and me.

After tons of reflecting, I realize that my job as a mother is regularly redefined by opposing views and challenges intended for my personal expansion. So, now I take deep breaths, find clarity, seek alignment, and proceed by asking more questions with an open mind and heart. I have learned that guilt and external viewpoints have no business in any parenting journey and to stop taking everything so darn seriously. The responsibility lies within me to create beliefs that are respectful and supportive. I can inspire my children to be self-reliant, compassionate, and ethical only when I model this behavior. Everyday remains a gift and a chance to grow.

Everyone who wants to be a great parent has that ability the moment they choose to stop blaming others, adjust belief systems that form limiting attitudes, and trust their intuition by forming mindful attitudes that are right for them and their family. Biological, adoptive, step, foster, single parents, multiple-parent families, grandparents, parents-to-be, relatives, teachers, pediatricians, and any person who influences a child's life should take the opportunity to transform their life in a more positive way by courageously assessing their values.

To be more in tune with modern day life, parents can make a commitment to be honest with themselves so they can unconditionally love their children. Those who re-define and secure personal ideals will protect themselves from external pressures that can easily influence their lives. Customizing foundations with beliefs that collectively empower support individual wholeness and development.

Parents achieve success by defining their own terms, at their own pace, with their own sense of purpose. A willingness to participate in an uncompromising journey of reflection, faith, and progressive beliefs can steer life and parenting in a positive direction. Personal growth is the greatest investment a person can make when venturing into parenting. Parents can begin to create new belief systems by imagining the parents they wished they had as children. Once that is defined they can reflect on how they parent and move toward their goals.

Use the following questions to help gain awareness and alignment between current belief systems and visionary parenting approaches.

- Name three words that describe you as a parent.
- Name three words your child would use to describe you as a parent.
- Is your current parenting belief system parallel to your truth?
- How does it guide your interactions and reactions?

- How can you use your life's challenges to improve your parenting now?

Answers to these questions can provide readers clarity for current belief systems. Once there is awareness there is greater ability to create shifts in conviction and personal parenting values that work. Parents who develop realistic beliefs systems create solid foundations that compliment *Wing It* ideas. An individual who envisions change is able to transform life into what they want and deserve. Personal belief systems that build balance and inspire change root life and parenting with enthusiasm and a courageous presence while equivalently prohibiting fear from hovering over decision-making.

Gently leaning into the process of shifting old belief systems and notions of how your parents screwed you up is powerful. It can also happen quickly depending on the experience and present need. Whenever circumstances no longer satisfy the essence of someone's individual journey, a simple change has to be made, steering toward a higher goal.

Individuals can honor that which brought them to wherever they are in their journeys by accepting the past and gracefully moving forward. An intellectual realization combined with heart wisdom and resilience of spirit can guide parents at any stage. Parents who step outside preconceived roles and disengage from passé beliefs form more harmonious existences. An influx of optimistic ideas can help push aside negative and unconstructive beliefs. The removal of inaccurate perspectives helps parents create new philosophies and sculpt belief systems full of promise that can be used to navigate life with ease and confidence.

So, *Did Your Parents Screw You Up?* Yes, and you can thank them for it, figuratively speaking of course, if it's not comfortable for you. In all honesty, once a person is able to recognize the benefit from any challenge experienced, they can easily trace a trait or strong suit that situation produced that strengthen their essence.

Whether a childhood experience made you overcome your worst fear or created a side to your personality that serves you well in the present day, parents tend to strengthen our resolve through negative or positive pushes and pulls. If your parents did screw you up, they did something that got you to this point successfully. After all, you are learning and evolving into a person who will achieve success in what's been coined the "hardest job on earth." You are an amazing person who is willing to be open and reflective on your own journey in parenthood, something that not everyone chooses to do. And because of that, and all that you are right now, you are able to parent differently and do your best in screwing your children up less!

Chapter 3

COURAGEOUS CONVERSATIONS

Kind words are short and easy to speak, but their echoes are truly endless.   - *Mother Teresa*

Ever wonder how much of what you say to a child really matters? Well, consider this, throughout my entire career from the thousands of people I have asked if they can recall a time when someone's words or action hurt them, every single person, no matter the age, can share a detailed, often emotionally stirring, story of when an adult said or did something that was so powerful that they continue to carry it in their souls to the present day. With this in mind, I share the urgency for parents, caregivers, teachers, and anyone who interacts with children to elevate their level of consciousness in communicating and understand that the magnitude of what is communicated can echo in children for a lifetime. People who communicate mindfully and wisely recognize the words and actions used have great potential to hurt or heal, put-down or uplift. The power is within each person at the very breath of a thought.

As an incurable optimist I used to believe that all people needed was love to make the world go round. But now, as a seasoned teacher and mother of five, I know for sure that if all ideas were communicated mindfully with loving intentions, the world would be a very different place. Words and expressions have the power to vibrate in people's souls, continually lingering in negative or positive interpretations, for days or even decades.

People who are courageously conscious with how they express themselves establish meaningful connections and open hearts. However, communication can also be the biggest divisor humanity has. Language more often divides people rather than unites and the perpetual words used affects individual success.

Communication, when well intentioned, thought out, and crafted cleverly, can initiate strength and courage, balance of mind and heart, and access to individual power. Once people learn to hold *Courageous Conversations* they will naturally manifest a higher level of awareness and can experience more productive exchanges, which foster greater respect and love.

Sharing in *Courageous Conversations* shape families and encourage more harmonious relationships. Good communication helps individuals structure their environments. Facial expressions and body language are vital aspects in interactions with children. They intuitively sense uneasy feelings or comforting messages and then react accordingly.

Those who remain intentional about what their faces and bodies are communicating along with the words they share construct a valuable consistency within relationships. Kids interpret both in an instant. Display conflicting verbal and non-verbal communication sends confusing messages. Children are natural-born intuitive interpreters.

Individuals who are alarmists or intrusive will convey fear to children, even without saying a word. In other words, what is expressed verbally as well as non-verbally communicates a message. Those who are looking to create loving environments with children can exhibit that in their communications simply by being mindful of what they are saying and what they are presenting to the outside world.

It is parents' responsibility to guide children by regularly initiating interactions with children. Once the subject matter needing discussion is pinpointed, parents can use the following four steps to communicate courageously (devoid of any pre-judgments or expectations) with their child: Step 1. Plan out the intent and goals in order to formulate thoughtful open-ended questions, Step 2. Find the appropriate time and a constructive way to begin the conversation, Step 3. Demonstrate skillful listening, and Step 4. Model good decision-making skills by including your child in the process.

Parents need to model good communication by being comfortable as both giver and receiver of information. People who remain objective and open to respecting the opinions and ideas that children share demonstrate that there is value in the relationship and teach good communication skills.

Courageous Conversations help people openly express how they envision themselves and their perceptions. They capture the spirit of one another. That is why parents must make the most of their conversations with their children.

Viewing others from different perspectives helps expand thoughts on equity and interests on both sides. The exchanges of ideas can reach a soul-to-soul connection that is genuine and powerful. Children naturally share authentic thoughts and communicate courageously, that is unless they are taught to not express what they know or feel. Children feel valued when others remain aware that they have something to share and give them the time and space to express themselves without judgment and minimal interference.

It is both people's responsibility to learn how to communicate well. However, parents need to provide guidance in learning the skills and gathering the tools needed to do so. Conversations need to have purpose, be meaningful, and in proportion to the child's age. The most valuable communications are fluid and loving, devoid of fears, suspicions or expectations.

Individuals who find a common rhythm and language with children usually have an easier time in sustaining good relationships. Younger children may draw as a way to communicate, or ask big life questions when playing games, while older children may prefer to text or write their feelings alone and share them on their own time. No matter the method, children who feel comfortable to express themselves are more likely to have higher self-esteem and more success in getting what they want throughout their life.

Courageous Conversations include a bit of planning on the adults part. Because, so often, adults are pre-wired to use a persuasive tone to try to protect rather than set a conversation up for an open conversation with an unknown outcome. It can be scary and take some practice to get comfortable. But, it is especially important for adults to learn how to hold safe spaces for children to be heard, places, free of criticism or retribution, where they can feel secure enough to express their needs, wants, feelings, and hopes at every age.

While some interactions may be dignified or defiant, confrontational or conspiratorial, elusive or evocative, and vary in tones, children have a right to be given the freedom they ought to have. Children who have the autonomy to express ideas gain a stronger sense of self and confidence in their core and learn how to express their feelings in a productive way. Children who are able to self-direct are ultimately more confident and happier.

The practice of *Courageous Conversations* helps relationships between parents and children move forward in a positive direction. Interactions can complicate or manipulate or can take on the form of being intimate and thoughtful. Most people are never taught how to communicate effectively as children, and grow up to be adults who are unaware of how to do it well.

An individual's composure and priorities flavor the process of expressing feelings. In order to create productive venues people should avoid using dismissive reactions or repetitive mini-lectures. Those approaches may seem like they work from an adult's perspective but, children need guidance more than anything, along with the freedom to think and make decisions for themselves in order for exchanges to be useful. Pressuring children to do or say things that are not genuine will lead to eventual rebellion or avoidance. Children, who feel they are not being heard, will search or gravitate towards people who they believe will listen. That's okay if the other person has their best intentions at heart. However, children who choose immature or uninformed people to discuss matters of importance with may lead them to risky outcomes.

Most parents realize the importance of sharing and communicating. They simply may lack techniques or fear for their child's well being if they let go of some control. *Courageous Conversations* involve confidence, questioning, listening, wait-time, and intuitive navigation that develops as people grow.

The challenge remains in the focus of communicating consciously. A young child's ability to learn new vocabulary is strongest through conversation. Therefore, parents' words and actions structure children's lives even at the earliest of stages. Baby talk, besides driving other adults nuts, can hinder a young child's communicative skills. Good communication keeps children learning about who they are, preserves their curiosities and passions about life, and shapes who they believe they can be. In the age of technology, people's mode of communication has changed dramatically. Face-to-face communication is not always people's first choice of how to correspond. For lack of time, convenience, or uneasiness, people have turned to technological interactions as much as possible. Instead of repelling these advances, parents can use them to their advantage.

Personal interactions will come in waves, whether electronically or physically, as people navigate through life. There are benefits for children to read messages and communicate technologically with parents. These tools can be powerful and productive in bridging gaps in relationships. Most parents appreciate the sense of security gained through technology by being able to contact their children in seconds no matter where they are. Often it's just a matter of conveying the facts that is important and, technology does just that.

Additionally, electronic communication grants parents the benefit of not having to witness the, often-animated body language or facial expressions children may display when they disagree. Now, isn't that reason enough to appreciate this progressive means of communication?

One struggle for today's generation may be to balance the use of technology with conscious, purposeful face-to-face communication. As the world progresses, people at every age can try to maintain a balance of meaningful communication and connectedness by eliminating claims of judgments, being kind and respectful, and discovering a common language.

Whatever the mode used, parents can teach children how to communicate by modeling good examples for them. Effective interactions do not happen when parents interrupt, multi-task, remain expressionless, or use sarcasm. Children interpret the emotional messages people around them express just as much, if not more, than what is being said. Naturally, they feel more than they think, and translate that meaning by being perceptive of the whole interaction. Children are born with an uncomplicated sincerity that allows them to communicate in a distinctively personal ways. They understand depth in responsiveness and react positively to parents who limit pre-judgments and remain positive in their communication with children. Parents simply have to be tuned-in to and ready for *Courageous Conversations* by remaining open and asking lots of questions.

Here are some guiding questions you can ask yourself to assess your communication skills. Think about your form, tone, and tendencies used in communicating.

- When do you communicate with your child?
- Who decides when it is time to communicate?
- How much time do you allow without interrupting?
- Are follow-up questions sincere with thoughtful intentions?
- When you communicate with your child, what does your facial expressions and body language display?
- How responsive are you when communicating with your child?
- How responsive are they?

Parents are victorious when they masterfully convey a respectful tone. Forced conversations, conflicting verbal and body language, or patronizing tones lead to devaluing a person's inner sense of knowing. Children cleverly rely on their other senses and intuition to express themselves. Parents can see this even with suggestive glimpses or lingering gazes.

Elevating the intent of communication incorporates active listening, empathy, thoughtfulness, accountability, and exercising a keen sense of purpose. Tremendous insight is gained when people listen to others the way they wish to be heard. By listening compassionately, souls connect and the moments shared shape relationships. Eliminating resistance to understand or be right organically builds bridges of happiness. Interactions, if loving and confident, will stand the test of time.

Today, parents who wish to grow children of character, people who are positive influences in this global world, should try using fewer words in their conversations and begin to listen more. Children need to feel appreciate for their wonderful ideas. Whenever moments of miscommunication arise, parents need to resist giving up or shutting down the lines of communication. And instead, find a way to bridge the gaps by emotionally involving themselves in different ways. Children are flexible and creative. Parents can learn a lot by following their lead and letting them direct the exchange of ideas.

Children need parents to connect more, engage in gentle touching, grounding, and safe explorations as they communicate. Parents who meet children at their level show respect, without speaking down to them. Children are tired of always looking up at adults and need adults to communicate with them on their level. This is a time when parents can stop assuming that they know their children before they really know their children. After all, children these days are learning and growing at considerable speed and are ever-evolving beings that expand more rapid than any other previous generation.

When challenging situations arise, try thinking about them from different perspectives and focus on building support. The path to communicating consciously and *Courageous Conversations* embrace awareness of others viewpoints. It provides a platform that fosters respect and inspires real-life teaching to come alive with purpose and meaning.

To learn the importance of listening and value all perspectives in interactions is not only a communication skill but, also a critical life skill. Individuals who do this teach understanding and elevate worthiness. Good communication is about remaining responsive and staying in touch with what is real. The task of doing this well promotes insight at a soul level. People who penetrate children's outer shells through true comprehension form strong bonds that build trust and influence. They embrace and foster the inquisitive nature of children. Young children constantly ask why. They remain inquisitive because they naturally want to get the most out of life. They yearn for meaning in life and in relationships. Nurturing this teaches them that they are valued. Ignoring or smothering curiosities hinders development.

It takes a great deal of attention to change a negative pattern of communication learned as a child. Children learn to be silent and lose their sense of self when they experience a devaluing upbringing. Others may rebel and communicate unsolicited exaggeration of opinions in an effort to gain attention. Parents' anger or fears hinder growth and limit viewpoints. Paying attention to the words and actions used in expressing oneself creates their reality. For example, if someone keeps saying they feel tired, or exhausted, or have no energy, they will create that in their subconscious and eventually, these elements will present themselves in life. Adults who reflect on their communication and form well-balanced spaces will manifest constructive habits of expression.

People value children by communicating in love even when life experiences and examples feel unloving. The greatest learning often happens in the most challenging of times when communication fails and the message is wronged. Whether there is a tantruming toddler or defiant teenager who cannot seem to communicate fluidly, a gap grows from the misunderstandings and the effort to fix things.

Effective communication is demonstrated with words, gestures, and tones free of angst or judgment. Communication is a two-way process with multiple dimensions and layers. An inner attitude of respect comes when people speak from a position of love. Parents who listen to the hopeful voices of children are reminded of the important lessons of life.

Just like a child's laughter reminds us to laugh. A question they ask a lot is "Why?" As many times as they ask, remember that there is a purpose. Often these moments trigger an awareness of unnecessary layers adults accumulate through life that are ready to be discarded. Take those repeated questions or phrases as gifts for you discover more about yourself, love more, and evolve. Children pick up on loving energy and feel respected when people are authentic, appropriate, and learn with them.

There is a process that helps people structure their approach in communicating that I learned from my friend and teacher, Karen L. Garvey. These four steps for communicating have helped me tremendously in structuring my conversations with my children and everyone in my life.

As a communicator I must...	*As a listener I need to...*
Know what I want	*Hear what is being said*
Choose language to express it	*Interpret what I heard*

Courageous Conversations take practice and a certain amount of dedication before individuals recognize immediate benefits. There needs to be trust in the process and faith in allowing the guidance of children through honest and open communication. This does work. There is a chance for miscommunications at any step, but also wonderful opportunities to connect with a deeper level of awareness to life experiences.

Here are some things that can go wrong during this four-step approach: The first step is about really figuring out what is ideally needed, both physically and emotionally. If someone is not clear about what they want, they will never be satisfied. Step two is all about finding the words and language that are both appropriate and inviting, a clear articulation of the want. Children, very often, do not have the language to express what it is they want. So, it becomes vitally important that adults model this step conscientiously, without being patronizing, so that children learn how to convey their feelings and ideas accurately.

For the role as a listener, the first step is about paying attention without interrupting or judgment in order to hear what is being said, even when negative words or tones are used. As people model better communicating, the level of positive communication by those around them will also increase. Interpreting what is heard is the final step in successful communication. What people want is not always easily articulated and being able to comprehend other people's ideas is a skill that takes developing. Parents have the great opportunity to practice this with their children at any age. Overall, the responsibility lies in the contribution and effort made in this path of communicating from both sides.

Communication in all of its forms is central in understanding life. From self-reflection to inspired creativity, communicating is the way people gain insight to the significance of life. The way in which adults communicate, whether interacting with someone who is three years old or twenty-three, will determine the effectiveness of the interaction.

Children remember more about how they felt in the overall conversational experience more so than the actually words uttered. Parents now have the chance to use that knowledge to help children become the best communicators possible. The power is in engaging in life, and motivating others to be their best through empowering and *Courageous Conversations*.

The more consciously individuals communicate, the greater the catalyst for positive movement in relationships. Adults who remain thoughtful about their intentions by delaying judgments, asking reflective questions, and venturing respectfully into an open conversation further their connections with children. Living honestly, fluidly, and genuinely attentive promotes respect and an evolved outlook among people.

Among humans, it is in the transferring of information that often causes confusion and flawed communication. Those who consciously communicate with clarity of intention, observation, and listening based on the concept that everyone is doing their best with no judgments, create greater understanding. These loving interactions are significant and bring about greater awareness and connections among people. Fusing awareness with intent behind the words that are communicated is vital for individuals who are raising or interacting with children.

Courageous Conversations, whether self-talking, amongst a family, or throughout a nation, are conduits for peaceful and positive living. This is essential in raising a well balanced, caring, and wise generation of children. People who evolve into peaceful communicators are more likely to produce creative solutions in life and for the world at large. Simply put, *Courageous Conversations* can enhance relationships and the connections people make in life, thus affecting one's path in reaching fulfillment.

Chapter 4

$$\mathcal{S}$$

RAISING
ROOTED & WINGED CHILDREN

There are two lasting bequests we can give our children.
One is roots, the other is wings.   *- Hodding Carter*

Parents today are raising a new kind of child. For this reason, parents who want to be successful in today's world must be highly evolved, intelligent, and more insightful than ever. They have more resources and carry greater responsibility to elevate humanity by raising loving, compassionate, cooperative children who are conscious of their purposes and strive for fulfillment.

Children these days certainly need roots and wings if they are to succeed. There is a fine balance between having children remain grounded, in natural harmony with their spirit, and fostering an ability to soar to their highest potential. Most challenges parents face today come as a result of fear-based attitudes. Parents need liberation from fabricated inferences that, in turn, will initiate a return to empowerment, ensuing greater chances for their children to thrive.

We live in a world where parents multi-task, focus on past mistakes and future scenarios, and are consumed by all types of unimportant matters that hinder their ability to live in the present moment. Modern life is packed with lots of time-suckers: parents work more, everyone tries to do it all, and children participate, more than ever, in a plethora of activities striving to be labeled "the best." The reality of it is, good parenting takes time, effort, and a very different perspective than most people actually have in raising children.

Humans are similar to all living things. Human beings need the balance of good foundations to grow their roots and the freedom to expand and mature. Providing children with roots signifies giving them opportunities to build confidence and a strong sense of themselves. This includes rock-steady support and a willingness to establish a safe place for children to be themselves. Children need to feel secure within themselves. They need a certain foundation framed with high expectations in conjunction with simple acceptance of what is.

Parents who plant their child's feet deep in the soil of consciousness and morality help them ascend with gumption and ambition to advance forward in life. This is a new way of life for families. Just as farmers tend lush soil with love and attention, parents have extraordinary opportunities to mindfully raise children for a world other generations only dreamed about. At its core, raising rooted and winged children is all about keeping them balanced by respecting the fact that they are powerful creators of their own life.

Like a tree grows mightily high up in the sky children are important reminders for adults to believe in the possibility of life. Parents have to support a rise in motivating children to reach fulfillment along their journey. They need to help children explore so they develop faith in their abilities and gifts they bring to this world. Wings on children represent their willingness to try new things and confidence within themselves.

The wings children develop strengthen their resolve and help them conquer insecurities and strive to be their best at all stages. Life provides opportunities for children to form their wings throughout childhood whenever they are given chances to voice their ideas and make choices they can learn from. Wings are not something parents give to their children when they turn a certain age. Rather they are developed and strengthened over time as children find their own power and gifts.

Parents who bravely re-frame beliefs and align with the spirits of their children support individualized development. To parent using dated techniques that may have been used in the past simply will not work long term with today's children. Using influences of fear to control children consequently robs parents of power and influence. Parents who incorporate the simplicity of the past with the abundance of contemporary perspectives will navigate parenthood with nobility and purpose.

Honoring the organic talents and gifts each child is born with along with the discovery of their intuition is ongoing. Parents can end struggles of trying to change children to fit their desired outcomes by unconditionally loving them. Unconditional love allows children to grow their wings and fly as high as they wish. Parents still need to guide children as they explore new ideas and create continuous experiences for their personal journey. This idea helps parents expand their effectiveness in raising spirit-conscious children, building confidence, courage, and character.

Parenting at every stage has its challenges. It takes confidence and flexibility to be a good parent. The instant a parent feels accomplished, routines, ideas, and techniques often need modification. Conversely, whoever said parenting couldn't be fun? It is thought provoking and challenging for even the most experienced parents but also can be rooted with optimism and pure delight when absent of pressure.

The way of *Wing It* encourages parents to adapt and grow throughout the parenthood process as well as release unnecessary burdens. Today's children are smarter, faster and more intuitive then any previous generation. Parents who take the time to listen with their hearts and embrace the process as it unfolds have an easier and more gratifying time. Parents who have clear purposes and an all-encompassing set of beliefs have a better chance of raising grounded children.

Children need parents who accept, respect, and love them. They need someone who teaches by example and nurtures connectedness in relationships. When children are not afraid of failure they will be more willing to explore the world around them. And it is better for children to discover life with people around them who can love and support them as they learn. Their excitement and curiosities about all that surrounds them helps them better understand life from a liberating viewpoint. Children who are free to explore are happier. They delight in discovery by purposely plunging into their preferences and interests in order to grow and expand on who they are.

Many people live in a culture where the focus about the future prevents the present from being fulfilling. Parents especially worry how soon children will turn over, crawl, walk, and talk. They may obsess about getting children into the best pre-schools, extra-curricular programs, awards they should receive, and so on. The emphasis is on receiving immediate approval rather than discovering the unique gifts each person brings to this wonderful earth organically.

More people need to realize that life is happening now. Their lives and those of their children are important right now, not when the milestone charts state nor when it is convenient or looks good for others. Conscious living throughout a child's journey trumps the way life is perceived by outsiders. Parents are not here to disturb their child's process but to appreciate, guide, and evolve. Parents may find at times that it feels like they are standing in the middle of a tornado. But, creating a life of self-discovery and exploration will foster a parenting experience that is loving, nurturing, and balanced, thus promoting roots and wings for their children.

I have been guilty of asking for more compliance from my children at times when they were being their independent, opinionated selves. Even at their youngest of ages they were pretty self-reliant and often continue to be impartial of other people's opinions, a socially unpopular manner that often perplexes adults. Those are all great traits but, as a mom, it took some growth on my part to be able to properly guide their intense spirits.

I cringe when I think of the few times I used the, "Do you know what people are thinking about your behavior?" as a ploy to get them to behave more obediently. As I evolved and began to listen to myself and put myself in the place of my children, I adjusted my parenting approach. I now use the answers from two questions to guide the way I raise my children: 1. What is the overall goal for my children? 2. Is my parenting approach consistent with those goals?

My objective is to provide my children with the roots and wings they needed to be independent and fulfilled. Whenever an individual action does not correspond to that goal, then I make a shift. This was the result when I became more individualized with my approach and listened to my intuition. I began to ask a lot more questions rather than regularly sharing my opinions to their experiences. I continue to approach parenting as an ongoing work in progress.

Parental preoccupation of what others might say or how they will react often hinders insightfulness to all that is good. It certainly influenced my past intentions. It frequently forces people to question their intuitive wisdom. *Raising Rooted and Winged Children* understands and accepts children for who they truly are – no preconceived rules about how they should be, think, feel, or act. Those who believe that, often take every interaction as an opportunity to awaken and understand a child's soul better.

This awareness helps children increase their self worth by generously allowing them to try things using their own intuition. Parents can help build confidence by supporting children to practice decision-making throughout childhood with the realization that those abilities don't magically appear when they reach adulthood. Individuals who continually insist that children do things their way, against a child's will, promote self-doubt and children who may have a harder time being confident in their decisions in life and as they grow.

While eating dinner at my parent's home many years ago, my husband and I decided to take our five children along with my niece out for ice cream. All the children decided to order the same thing, two scoops of cotton candy ice cream with gummy bears on top. Who knew gummy bears could be considered a topping? Nonetheless, we allowed each child to order whatever she or he wanted and we had a great day that my children still remember.

It quickly became apparent that the majority of little ones experienced a massive sugar reaction about half way back home from the trip to the ice cream store. We all made it back to my parents' home safely. The next thing I remember was seeing the other adults' eyes popping out of their heads. There, standing in the center of the living room, stood my youngest child, two weeks shy of turning three, using my father's cane as a pole to dance around as she was passionately singing "hoedown" from the Hannah Montana movie.

Earlier in my parenting journey I would have been mortified, or hastily turned off the song every time it came on the radio, maybe even lectured her on the appropriateness of her moves for fear she was destined to become a stripper by the age of 15! Instead, there I stood, paused for a while as I silently asked myself, "What does this really mean?" I erased all the preconceived fears and judgments and realized my overall goal is to raise independent, happy, confident children. This reflection helped me understand she was simply expressing herself and it had nothing to do with me. I was able to rejoice in her enthusiasm for listening to her soul.

In the last twenty years parents faced some frightening isolated incidents in a world that sometimes seems more harmful than loving. Living in a global world that presents limitless connections, and ever-changing lifestyles parents certainly need a different mindset than that of the past. In order for parenting to be forward-thinking and absent of a motives based on fearful perceptions, parents can begin to look at the bigger picture. This entails coming to the realization that there is no possible way to protect children from all unknowns.

If parents worry about the uncertainties, they will be likely to attract fearful unknowns to their experiences. Providing children with substantial roots and wings alleviates the pressure from parents feeling that they must get a grasp on all that is new and uncharted. When there is a focus on allowing children live to their fullest potential, free of anxiety they will steadily grow into independent and responsible people. People who provide children support along with permission to become the most they can be are *Raising Rooted and Winged Children.* Cultivating that strong balance is what children of today need.

There are many periods in history when parents gave children too many roots and not enough wings. Throughout history, parents focused on the holding down children and prevented them from reaching their potential. They dictated their children's futures without any consideration of their potential. Roles were specified by necessity and individual interests or abilities were rarely regarded as valuable. Distinctive aspirations were squashed, a trickle-down effect, which caused dreams to get pushed aside and disconnect to develop.

In the past, children followed in the footsteps of their families. There was little exploration of individual gifts and beliefs were hinged on traditional practices. Children grew up often in turmoil with personal insight that conflicted with societal ideals. Families were driven by group needs more so than individual aspirations and possibilities. The focus was on providing strong roots and remaining firmly planted in the soil of the family, never venturing away.

Over the past few centuries, children were thought of as vulnerable, little people that needed protection from a big, scary world. There were many alarming stories in the media about tainted candy, deadly diseases, kidnappings from men in vans, ramped drug use, and school shootings. Parents became reactive and consumed with keeping children safe at all costs.

Often, people felt powerless over the mass media's frenzy over scary incidents. There were immediate remedies to allergens in foods, solutions to academic frustrations, eradication of risky toys, and the Internet consumed parents with fears of misuse and exploitation. As a response to parents' guilt at both having to work, children became over-scheduled and under-nurtured. With society's scare tactics at the forefront, neighborhoods changed and children lost their ability to explore liberally and play. In addition, parents forgot to bestow grounding aspect along with freeing prospects children so desperately need in childhood to become successful adults.

Times have certainly changed from when I was a little girl. Children were basically scared into doing what parents felt were the "right" things. Sure parents "made" children, for the most part, listen to them in doing what was expected, but think about what that really taught children. Most adults, when reflecting on their own childhood, can recall feeling frightened, guilty, or shamed. Traditional parenting paradigms were quite linear and included one way of doing things instead of providing an emphasis on appreciating a child's whole being.

Parents opted to rule anxiously over children, which then gave way to a hands-off approach as children grew into adolescents and teenagers, for fear of repeating the mistakes their parents made with them. Trepidations formed an artificial scaffold in parenting. Socially acceptable trends included feeling an obligation to micromanage children, arranging multiple activities, and an over-concentration in brain development at earlier and earlier ages. Parents were (and many still are) incessantly "preparing" children for the next step.

In more recent decades, courage and optimism have burst the bubbles that permeated past societal parenting approaches giving way to more comprehensive ways of raising children. We stand at the dawn of a conscious new parenting age. There is a modern day path of mindful insight that helps develop optimistic principles that can drive families toward shared prosperity.

Conscious, respectful parenting facilitates better development and harmony for children in the long run. The current culture of the world is more complex, is ever changing, and can certainly be considered scary at times. In light of humanity's unfamiliar responses children may be given too many wings without enough roots from parents who are unsure of what to do.

There needs to be stability between the roots and wings parents give children. The past proves the importance of giving young children both roots and wings to prepare them for real life in today's modern world. Now all parents have to figure out is how to provide children with just the right amount of roots to keep them grounded and wings to allow them to grow to be independent thinkers and doers.

The *Wing It* philosophy allows parents to mindfully adjust the lens on parenting this new group of children. The strategies help people to recognize individual beauty and hope within children, to appreciate the whole child void of fearful attitudes. Parents can value the significance of bracing children while sanctioning them in an independent union of mind, body and soul. This present day emerging parenting approach includes a respect for everyone's individual journey, the encouragement of personal evolution, as well as an appreciation for the global world.

Today parents know better and are less bound to the traditions of past generations. Society as a whole has become more aware. When parents realize the ramifications of not paying attention to children's social-emotional well-being and admit the harmful outcomes of over-scheduling and competitive their approaches can change. And with the support of strategies like those presented in this book, that are custom developed by each individual family, parents will continue to awaken to personal potential and that of their children.

Encouraging the development of roots and wings in children support the way parenthood of today needs to change. This awareness can produce a broader range of differentiation in parenting styles, ones that are inclusive, accepting, and loving. Parenting that is successful takes an unhurried yet inquisitive look, which remains direct, ambitious, and liberating. It is a compelling way to launch children into the future as they follow their individual dreams with passion and hope.

In today's world, parents can take the time to be present and accepting. The difference between the ordinary and wakeful parents is that the latter do not lose their identity while on their journey. Wakeful parents are highly insightful and fluid in their position. As they grow in awareness and love, they are able launch more independent children and recognize their wisdom. They form brilliant foundations of acceptance, guidance, engagement, and unconditional love. They avoid smothering the evolution of possibilities for the next generation.

Today's parents can be innovators in building families with new perspectives and an absence of limiting beliefs. This is a time of abundant possibilities with children who are more insightful than any previous generation. If trust, goodness, faith, and worthiness color the way parents raise their children, then they are bound to experience bliss in parenting. People must consciously choose to evolve and honor the natural sense of wonderment for a joyous life with children who are confidentially rooted in their beings and winged so they can explore and reach a higher realm of understanding.

At times in history, from the iron-fist approach to attachment parenting to outsourcing parenting to service providers, and drilling via enrichment videos to over-permissiveness we see how parents can be a bit confused on how to accomplish successful rearing of children. Today parents have more access to resources then ever to evolve into exceptional role models for children. After all, children are fun loving spirits to be enjoyed, not broken down. Bow to the challenges of providing opportunities where children can grow and root themselves into people who are open to possibilities and seek enlightenment.

The truth is that all parents want to raise great children. An overwhelming majority of parents try their best. Present day parents need to set new standards embedded with optimism for themselves, their parenting, and their lives. As a result of the unstable world that surrounds us, there needs to be a balance more than ever. *Raising Rooted and Winged Children* incorporates symmetry to raising children as harmonious beings that can change the entire advancement of their generation.

Now is the time to work hard on providing children the ability to interact with the world as their own person, to expand their confidence, and competence to interact as dynamic life contributors. Children need to feel safe and empowered, and productive. Children need support from parents to rocket higher and farther, reaching their own climactic experiences.

Honor in the natural importance of balance between having both roots and wings for a well-balanced, fulfilled life sets this generation apart. Parents who understand children from the inside out and get the importance of alignment worry less over potential dangers in the world and allow children to grow well all in an effort to encourage children to explore their full potential. By bringing attention to parenting and championing children to branch out in life and re-discover their greatness, is to live life as it was meant to live.

Parents can learn a lot from nature and especially in the wonderment of trees and the lessons they are here to teach. Just as the fullest, strongest, most beautiful tree is a source of strength, so are our children. Trees are inspiring just as children are. Trees show resilience in the stormiest of times. They are flexible and always belong just where they stand, being careful to bend with the ever-changing winds. They remind us to reach high towards the stars as stunning testaments of nature. Parents, for centuries have been concentrating on helping children reinforce their roots. Now it is time to focus on balance and let them grow naturally toward endless possibilities.

Parents who believe in the *Wing It* philosophy can envision themselves as the powerful trees that birds fly to in order to be safe, or find their grip, or build homes near by, or take moments to pause in between their journeys. The trees where birds find it safe to return but not dependent on, the places they to fly from with ease in order to explore their environments and abilities.

The leaves on the trees allow sunlight to shine through so that birds are able to see the world and be reminded of all the beautiful points of light. These mighty trees sway and bend with the winds that teach birds to remain flexible as they experience life. Then, when the birds are ready, they take flight by spreading their wings and venturing out to discover the wonderful world. All this happens as the trees keep growing in their own direction, at their own pace, and towards their own purpose.

Chapter 5

BUILD YOUR VILLAGE

What does a child need? Love beyond all else.
Unconditional love and acceptance combined with gentle
and consistent discipline and guidance. They need a
balanced diet. They need to have their minds and their
bodies engaged and stimulated. They need quiet and
security. They need respect. They need their soul songs
heard so that their individual beauty can be honored.
- Karen L. Garvey -

The current culture of our world highlights the importance of people investing time in creating personal constructions of well-balanced environments and relationships. *Build Your Village* considers the powerful significance of producing culturally receptive surroundings, ones that support individual visions for life. All human beings need villages. No one exists alone.

The villages individuals create have profound effects on how they live. A key responsibility when becoming a parent is to be more mindful of one's surroundings. The villages parents structure prepare both themselves and their children for navigating the world at large. This draws a parallel to the thinking of what you do for yourself, you do to your child, and what you do for your child, you do to yourself.

Harmonious communities propel an increased energy in all aspects of life. When surroundings are created carefully and considerately individuals prosper, consequently strengthening the whole village. As parents design their circumstances, they must trust the overall philosophy of "it takes a village" by allowing new interactions, development of relationships, and the associations within the village that benefit the individuals as well as the group.

So how do parents craft nurturing, loving, ideal places for their own families? They begin by taking an honest soul-probing account of who they want to be and what type of life experiences they desire. They remain intentional in their undertaking of designing the most dynamic lives for themselves and their families. This includes the five essential building blocks for living: culture, people, environment, tasks at hand, and life lessons. They set themselves up for success by existing in their own truth and walking in authentic paths. They stay attentive to people around them and to the situations generated. They recognize how a parent's village greatly affects his or her children and their life experiences as well.

Modern day parents value relationships which are enriched through meaningful experiences and understand importance of consciously shaping venues where they feel safe to be themselves and present with their children, not in glorified cliques or gatherings that are emotionally tiresome or filled with judgment. Build Your Village grants significant opportunities for parents to initiate synchronicity and joy in their lives by following a contemporary blueprint relevant to today's families.

Gauging progress within geography, religion, culture, communities, and the world will help parents gain insight to one's personal village including who they surround themselves with, their personal self worth, the experiences they attract, their abilities, and their visions. From the outside, some aspects may be perceived as negative due to a unique stance. There is no right or wrong perception. It is simply about what works within a particular village. Your charge as a parent is to create an environment that aligns with your parenting principles and goals.

Villages respond to what is needed by the members in it. Gaining personal clarity helps create a vision of ideal environments each person desires. Whatever a person thinks, feels, and believes will manifest in to reality. The time is ripe for parents to courageously generate purposeful arrangements as they grow modern day families and navigate life.

First, parents can do their best in evaluating their experiences within their current communities. If there exist any limitations or something does not align with their parenting belief system, there will be a negative impact on their progress. Next, parents can use contrast to their advantage in order to observe what is missing from their life. Conflicts erect stirring feelings with aspects that do not match a person's intention. This awareness is about getting real and focusing on what circumstances people want in their life. Finally, parents need to take inventory to make sure they have enough space for the people and experiences they desire. A de-cluttering of superfluous beliefs, people, places, and routines is in order to welcome more specific, mature happenings they want to embrace.

So how do parents re-design their surroundings gracefully? They erect distinctively supportive villages with constructive parenting philosophies that inspire parents and encourage everyone's greatness to emerge. This is more than adjusting a belief system. It is a plan in purpose where parents gain awareness of their culture, consciously assemble a loving community of people, build encouraging environments, and remain mindful of experiences with their children that steer what is best for their family.

Wing It parenting assembles specific steps that can be taken to be successful. Each parent is like a chef being asked to create the best, most flavorful, scrumptious, delightful cake - only their masterpiece is the village, a marvelous environment that allows their family to flourish. The essential ingredients of a village include a healthy balance of culture, people, environments, tasks at hand, and life lessons. Just as with any fabulous formula, there are no limits to what parents choose to include. The individual determines the quality of components for his or her own village. People who confidently build and nourish well-balanced villages by including the key elements will have a higher propensity toward true fulfillment for themselves and their families.

The Fundamental Elements of *Build Your Village are...*
CULTURE
Let us begin with the simple fact that everyone has a *culture*. How people define their *culture* is all up to them. This global world provides a fascinating diversity with an incredible opportunity to understand the richness in the human tapestry of the world, an invaluable life lesson for all people. The common thread that holds humanity together is the optimistic plan for cooperation and acceptance.

This new generation of children is exposed to more variety than any other. The cultures that exist within each person are also magnificent. Their acceptance and willingness to appreciate this diversity will guide them to a new paradigm of building a better world. The importance of people being able to see themselves in others is how it all comes together and supports dynamic life experiences.

There exist two levels of *culture* within every human being. There is surface culture as well as deep culture. Surface *culture* is a small portion of what is observed in any individual. It is like the tip of the iceberg that exposes itself above the sea for everyone to notice. However, that only makes up about 10% of the actual iceberg. The surface *culture* in humans includes clothing, food, shelter, religion, education, lifestyles, etc. The things that are easily visible to the outside world. I like to call it the "window dressing" of humanity. Surface *culture* is the information that is almost always used inaccurately to categorize people because it in no way represents the entire essence of any individual, just as the tip of the iceberg only represents a small portion of the whole.

The deep *culture*, on the other hand, is the majority of who someone really is. It is similar in proportion to the bulk of the iceberg concealed underneath the water's surface. This is where people house their opinions, beliefs, desires, fears, reasons behind their thinking and doing, and all the details of their authentic self. Often people resist sharing their deep culture for fear of being exposed or judged.

Deep *culture* has to do with mind, body, spirit wisdom and the how and why people navigate through life the way the do. It explains why some things irk people while other things roll on by without notice, and why one child may be an extrovert and risk-taker while a sibling is withdrawn and hesitant in new encounters. When a person uncovers their real spirit inside their core they move closer to defining their true self. *Culture* at both levels must be considered and valued. Understand that children are also their own people endowed with unique personal cultures of their own that will vary. A parent's job is to simply allow and accept all that a child's *culture* communicates as she or he changes and grows.

Children define their primary *culture* by the main experiences they are exposed to. Then, at later stages, through personal inquisitiveness they formulate an individual all-encompassing personal culture that changes and morphs into an independent representation of their experiences and preferences. Therefore, it is immensely valuable for parents to provide variations in life whenever possible.

Depictions of multi-faceted lifestyles will strengthen a child's will to discover more about themselves and develop into a wise, well-rounded, compassionate human being. Children are brave and clever enough to define their cultures much more quickly than adults. Children are born as curious and natural explorers. They are often willing to try new things and study something different which generates a growth in mindset.

Honoring your *culture* is fundamental as is exposing children to other cultures, all in an effort to enrich lives. The world is a wonderful arena of beauty and abundance and exists for humans to explore and enjoy. People are the creators of their lives, which offers endless possibilities. This may include blending traditions or languages, foods, music, religion, education, lifestyle, or expectations from one's primary *culture*, which they were born into, with new experiences that people take on as adults that often guide them to form unique cultures closer to their individual essence. As each person matures so does his or her *culture*.

Cultures transform as people grow, travel with various groups, share in diverse experiences, and explore new places. Parents who encourage the evolution of their child's culture by nurturing their innate sense of wonder about others and life will help them unveil limiting perspectives. Successful parents nowadays are those who are innovative. They focus on creating opportunities for the expansion of their personal cultures as they respect and accept of the uniqueness of their child's.

Parents can create uplifting experiences through exposure to people and encounters that spark core interests. Parents who reflect on the influence surrounding children in the books, activities, people, practices, and stories they are exposed to can utilizing situations as springboards to communicate unifying messages and increase appreciation. Everyone has a *culture* and it is up to parents to help cultivate and inspire children to shape relationships that fundamentally support loving principles.

When a parent highlights a child's own cultural identity through connections that reflect real life they will gain a greater understanding of themselves. Parents' beliefs and reactions are key in determining how much children learn to trust in themselves. Fear-based ideas deeply influence a child's unwillingness to explore and accept different facets in their *culture*. Parents must caution themselves to not obstruct opportunities for children due to reluctance within their own background. Rather, they can structure experiences that highlight real life circumstances featuring perseverance, resilience, and enlightenment. Then those attributes can be highlighted in how children shape their cultures.

PEOPLE

Next, let us discuss the magnitude of importance the *people* and relationships that love without conditions as well as those that produce challenges have in people's lives. Relationships are the radius for guiding people and maintaining wellness in villages. Everyone's assembly of *people* contains different characters and conditions.

Observing and listening to oneself and those within the family unit in order to assess how relationships are emerging within their present village is crucial. Certainly there needs to be careful consideration for family member's needs by selecting *People* and things that embrace their agreed values. However, parents wanting to have a clear focus on formulating the finest group of *people* must take care of themselves first ("air mask over your face first before your child" concept for a greater chance of survival). In this instance, not only should parents expect to survive amongst others but thrive with good motivation and proper support as they evolve.

All *people* who live their lives with significance and purpose cultivate meaningful interactions within their villages. We all need help from our friends to create a good tribe vibe. Modeling that for children is the conduit for success in future relationships.

Once parents feel they are in a good place personally, they can begin to build supportive communities of *people*. First, there needs to be a review of relationships with people presently in their life: partners, siblings, parents, in-laws, neighbors, friends, co-workers, cousins, babysitters, clergy, etc. Parents can ask themselves, "Are my current relationships the best they can be? Am I the best I can be when I am with them?" If the answers to either of those questions is no, then there is apparent work that needs to be done.

People within a village can be valuable agents of truth and can help authentically gauge personal progress. Parents who are open to opportunities for discovery within themselves and others will have more of a reflective progression. Consider that every single human being is doing the best they can within his or her level of understanding can help lessen judgments of others. Once that idea is received for sure, it can help people surrender any quests to help change other *people* and focus on themselves. The genius of this understanding is that parents can concentrate on their own evolution with out trepidation or guilt about decisions or journeys made by others, including those of their own children.

All humans naturally construct a circle of *people* whose company and friendships steer them in certain directions. Parents can knowingly choose people who encompass wonderful traits sought after in life and elevate relationships. To shield themselves and their children from unconstructive relationships means individuals are actually honoring themselves. They can release partnerships with those who encumber their lives. No one should be there by default.

Any body can free themselves of *people* and circumstances that weigh them down or hamper happiness. Everyone has an inner compass which helps determine the relevance of the *people* who exist in his or her present day life. Nobody's purpose in life includes providing fertile ground for the burdens or negative journeys of others. Also *people*, in general, should never allow anyone into their village who is hurtful. If they come attached to someone they love than there needs to be clear parameters by which they are allowed access in the village.

The *Build Your Village* concept stems from the importance of allowing others in your circle of influence. There is something profoundly flawed with incessantly accepting negative *people* that lead to unconstructive circumstances in one's life. If this is a pattern that you recognize, then a re-examination of your belief system and your circle of influence is crucial. It can be about simply letting go of anyone who depletes them of time, energy, or love and willfully engage with wonderful people that share empathy, enthusiasm, and mutual respect.

Everyone's village is so individualized. That which defines our uniqueness is the thread that binds us all together. And *people* show appreciation and remain respectful of individual values by modeling constructive interactions within the group.

Remaining careful not to wall themselves in because of mistakes or mistreatment by others can help *people* stay open to love and positive experiences. When parents are receptive to other people and their love, they magnetize others who possess those characteristics as well. Parents are responsible to design villages that are liberating, nurturing, safe, inspirational, and loving for them and their children.

I was not always mindful in constructing my circumstances as I am today. I went through periods where I surrendered my power to *people* around me. I sometimes allowed *people* who were negative, critical, wearing, and impatient and not coming from a place of love in my immediate circles of influence. I felt an obligation to be loyal to certain family and friends...probably out of guilt. However, once I awoke and matured, I shifted my principles and automatically became happier.

This change in thinking caused a positive transformation in the composition of people within my village. Life with my children became easier and I felt less anxious in general. Now, as I honor my spirit I attract in *people*, things, and experiences that produce joy, peace, and hardy laughter. Today, guilt plays no role in my choices of *people* I spend my life with or in the assembly of my village. Raising children does take a village. My village includes *people* who sanction cooperation, love, peace, and respect. And an equally important notion is to consciously welcome diversity so my children experience life from a global perspective.

Different types of *people* in life help others to expand into better people even if they are not perceive at first as gifts, hence the annoying neighbor or in-law, the judgmental friend or exhausting child. The best way to find out if a relationship needs to be severed or maintained is based on if you are able to find the advantage of the lessons in those that presently surround you. It is important to try and search for balance within every union before ending a challenging relationship. Conditions can change the moment you adjust your outlook on life and are able to define parameters that feel right for you. If similar traits appear in new *people* you meet then there is an existing lesson you need to learn. Get to know yourself enough to make relationship decisions based on what you are able to give and receive at the time. Acceptance and positive subsequent actions will help change any patterns, and, at the end of the day, elevate a family's circumstances.

Consideration of the overarching energy of relationships parents have in their present day life is imperative. The process of observing and defining needs and wants may feel contrived as you begin, but as you sift, sort, and avail yourself of the best *people*, your life will feel more authentic. There are always choices to be made and when *people* take on the role of parent, there must be generous reflection of the impact decisions have on the overall wellness of the family.

Stress and worry about the emotional layers of others restricts happiness. It is a choice to remain connected to or to detach from the *people* in your current village. You get to choose. Be honest and insightful with your choices. Move away, both physically and emotionally from people who do not support your growth.

At the same time accept, without judgment, that everyone needs different *people* around them at various times in their lives. Use your energy to build the perfect community of human beings that honor your values and principles. The best way parents can build self-reliance within their children is by modeling real-life skills and concepts that will radically impact children's creations of their own villages as they grow.

As a result of a parent's guidance, a child will recognize the strength and wisdom in surrounding him or herself with *people* who travel peacefully and productively in their childhood. This will teach them cooperation, acceptance, and how to make good decisions in their future as well. However, they need consistent guidance in crafting their surroundings.

As children get older, they need to continue to learn by doing. They are very capable and should be encouraged to form their own relationships within their villages. Parents need to stimulate, not control, children's decisions. Controlling children simply disempowers them and stifles their ability to be confident with their decisions. Allow them to have autonomy as they develop, choose friendships, and form their own human connections. It is about fostering independence and leadership attributes beginning at an early age.

Children don't spontaneously learn to be great decision-makers at age eighteen or twenty-one. They are born innately intelligent. Parents simply have to cultivate their strengths and provide guidance from the earliest point in life while trusting in the *Build Your Village* process.

People will often come into a child's life to reflect something back to them, helping them evolve. Parents have to allow that process to happen. They must permit other people to do their job in being their teachers, and play the roles that their child needs at that time.

Trust in the *Build Your Village* process and refrain from being over-protective, which prevents children from learning life-lessons. Release worries and have faith in your child, that they will develop their own relationships with *people* and learn how to use their intuition to become responsive to others in order to find their own strengths and limits. Parents cannot teach their children everything. Life does not work that way, and those who try rob their children of experiences that would otherwise launch potential growth. Supportive strategies will come from real-life observations made throughout their lives. Use those moments to guide and teach the importance of awareness. *People* who work together collectively evolve. Sculpt your village into a place where you and others work toward a common goal of communicating love, acceptance, and faith.

ENVIRONMENT

The next part of *Build Your Village* is about creating a physical setting that is uplifting and feeds the spirit of you and that of your child. Parents have the power to change the entire *environment* in which their family lives. The sheer amount of time spent in your personal surroundings establishes the importance of generating a place of pure potential love. Everyone everywhere has the choice and power to transform their *environment*. Big, cold, dark places or small, cluttered spaces can all be modified making room for a setting that supports happiness and wellness. Purposely create venues that are satisfying to your heart, mind, and soul.

When we decided to have children, my husband and I made a conscious choice not to turn our world into "kiddie land." Likewise, there is nothing wrong with parents who dwell in the materialistic representation of all that is child-like if that works for them. In order for me to feel good and whole, I choose to design a home that belongs to everyone. Each family member has his or her own space and things they enjoy in a respectful manner.

Additionally, I intentionally created an *environment* in a style that works for me, first as a woman, then as a mother. My surroundings are colorful and calming with beautiful furnishings in fabrics and materials that are durable; there are framed photographs of our family life displayed throughout our home along side finger paintings and purchased art from our travels. A mixing and matching of real life treasures makes all of us feel like valued members of the family. I have my space, my husband his, and the children have their places to use and live in. Everyone feels comfortable and respected in our home.

Begin by carving out a sacred space for you in addition to your bedroom. Whether that is a corner in a bathroom to meditate, a favorite chair to read in, or an outdoor area to exercise. Parents deserve spaces that are easy, clutter-free, and contain only things that they love. It is important that they make conscious choices about colors, surfaces, and styles they prefer. Choosing feel-good things that warm their hearts and bring smiles to their faces is what having a space of your own means.

A parent's bedroom should be their principle sanctuary, a place where they can be surrounded by serenity and peace. Whatever that looks like and feels like to each individual. Items displayed in their bedroom are the last things seen before someone goes to sleep and first things they see each morning as they wake, so it is very important that they are uplifting and inspirational in nature. It is essential that a parent's room reflects who they are and the wondrous spirit inside them. If it is valued, it becomes a space that honors them and there whenever it's needed.

At every age, people need a space for themselves that represents who they are. Be sure to communicate with your child to help them design their living areas as well. Listen to them without judgment and allow them to express themselves in their spaces. Have them join you in decisions about what feels right in their room. Remember there is always room for options and compromise; it is up to you to present things in a respectful manner.

Parents can ask lots of questions and listen for direction. Buy books and toys that are free of biases and represent the global world. Share in an assortment of experiences that are unique in an effort to help your child discover what excites their spirit. Your willingness to give them autonomy will be appreciated and remembered.

Respect their space. Nourish and display their innate creative ideas. Designate places in your home where your children have independence to be themselves, to express themselves and discover things with all their senses. Even a small closet can be the greatest of adventures for young children. Relish the moments of pure imagination and encourage play, exploration, inspiration, and creativity as long as you can.

Being in nature is vital and freeing. It is the ultimate playground that often needs little improvement. Children understand the magnificence of life existing in the world whenever they are free to explore in nature. Understanding all living things are connected catapults an appreciation of life's magnificent gifts that can foster growth at all levels for parents and children alike.

As a family, take time to look outside the walls of your home to the outdoor landscape. Join with your child to explore nature and build harmonious surroundings together. Planting a garden is an excellent way of making your *environment* beautiful and also a chance to be present with your child, observant of the wonderment of nature. Touch everything that surrounds you mindfully to heighten awareness.

Self-awareness is a natural conduit to connect and expand with the organic world around you. The world is full of beautiful textures, colors, and depth that represent completeness. Pause to observe and breathe in all that exists in front of you. Children are great believers in the power of nature and often remind us that life is in the present, in the here and now. Parents building villages should take cues from the wisdom in children's unhurried pace as they openly discover nature's splendor and the greater *environment* on earth.

Allow your home *environment* to be a welcoming canvas for everyone's creative expressions. When parents tune in and sanction rather than restrict, wonderful opportunities arise, full of meaningful learning for everyone. Remain aware how outside influences have the potential to change a family's *environment*. The external world, media, and collective ideas can easily seep into your village and impact your surroundings. Parents should avoid coloring their villages with blaring misconceptions or narrow views of the real world. Make a conscious effort to create *environments* that value innovation and diverse perspectives. Parents who create respectful communities of people in conjunction with designing harmonious physical spaces encourage healthy progress for their entire family.

TASKS AT HAND

Make time your ally and everything becomes easier. There is a time for everything. The moment you allow time to be on your side you will accomplish the *Task at Hand* contentedly. People who worry about being late, attract that in to their life creating a self-fulfilling prophecy.

Parents especially need to savor life's precious instances, no matter how insignificant they may seem. Unrehearsed events are often those that bring the greatest impact. Hold on to moments with children long enough to delight in the exquisite gifts offered therein. How you set yourself up for success as a parent is all up to you. This practical part of creating positive experiences and balancing expectations should consist of enjoyment together with accomplishment.

Whatever the goal, individuals must consider the *Task at Hand* and prepare for it. Each day is the chance to enjoy life, not to be viewed as a bunch of jobs needed to get done as quickly as possible. Life is not a race and no one gets a trophy for getting the most things done. The prizes in life are the moments of pure bliss when people take that instant to pause and enjoy the marvel of being present with others.

The most prevalent problem expressed by parents has to do with time and patterns in behavior, that is, parents' negative behaviors that cause children's negative reactions that "wastes" time. A child's disapproving behavior ultimately results in parents' displays of frustration or anger directed back toward the child who is only doing the best they can with what they have been taught.

Once the paradigm is acknowledged, there can be a shift in perception and the dynamics of the relationship will change, bringing forth fresh, new outcomes. Most of the trials and tribulations in parenthood have to do with alarming ideas that prevent parents from moving forward and changing unconstructive practices.

As mentioned earlier, parents these days often say "no" a lot more than they say "yes." This is based on a lack of time, patience, or fear-based beliefs. They are not using innate wisdom or non-judgmental attitudes, which ultimately results in parenting inconsistencies. Being authentic ensures that you will be consistent and that engenders trust. Recognition of one's own feelings can lead to confronting fears and eliminating them. That's the only way to conquer a fear – stare straight at it so you can move passed it.

Once parents identify their fears, they can actively dissolve stress and develop more positive positions to parent from. When a person tunes into the present moment and releases fears of past or future thoughts, they are able to redirect themselves into mindfully living with children, saying "yes" more to life, and experience joy in the midst of all the tasks they perform.

Task at Hand is the practical management piece of parenting. First off, the not-so-secret trick is to do things that are age appropriate and engaging for children at times when they are in a positive state of mind. This seems simple enough but it does not hurt to remind parents. This rings true in spite of age, whether we are referring to an infant, toddler or teenager. They are all people who deserve respect and consideration just as much as adults do.

Keeping that in mind, if there is a choice on timing, make your plans during the part of the day when your child is most agreeable. Lighten up and try to make the task fun. Almost any situation can include something in it that can be engaging to a child if considered ahead of time.

Communicating mindfully in order to clearly describe what you expect and ask them questions before an event to ease anxiety or misunderstandings. At any age, children appreciate being considered and respected for what they want to do. Food shopping after a child has eaten and is well rested is smart, as is involving them in the errand. Choosing a family friendly restaurant and bringing along toys and table games for your child is also a simple way of setting up for success. Answering the phone is also an automatic magnet for a child of any age to gravitate toward you the moment you reach for the phone. Think of a way to get them engaged in something while you are making your call such as a bag of fun stuff by the phone that you can take out for their entertainment while you speak.   And older children should get choices of how and when they need to be involved in the tasks. Modeling the concept that there are always options helps children grow to be more flexible and understanding.

Most importantly, at times when you are physically responsible for your child, be present with them and be in the moment with what is happening. Abstain from worrying about past issues or anticipating future problems. Be there physically and emotionally. There are always choices. People who take on the role of parenting in today's high-tech and high stress world must consciously disengage themselves from modern-day advances and disruptions in order to responsibly remain present and authentically connect with their children. Be realistic in your own expectations and those of your child's, and let that awareness help you respond in positive ways, making shared moments special.

Parents need to remain fluid and flexible in order for children to recognize that anything is possible and life is good. Children can surprise you with their resilience and their tenacity. They are born open and therefore have greater awareness in sensing frustration and anxiety in others. Calmness combined with ease grants parents an improved time with children. I find that whenever I spend real time with my child, engaged in an activity uninterrupted, they are respectful when I have something to do that is important to me.

Savoring the moments together makes children feel valued so there is no need for them to crave reactive attention. There are always those unpredictable events that cannot be planned around a good time which could result in some resistance but not necessarily. Avoid the pitfall of anticipating the worst-case scenario. By thinking optimistically and planning thoughtfully, parents give themselves a greater probability to be successful in their goals. Children have an innate astuteness for knowing when something is important to their parents and more often than not, do actually try to do their best to cooperate.

One story that comes to mind is the time I was pregnant with my fifth child and needed to go for my six-month check up at the gynecologist. My husband did not get home in time to watch our four children so, there was no other choice then to bring them with me.

Clearly it was not an ideal situation, especially with boys ages two and four who loved anything having to do with the word naked or privates! I could have crumbled that instant. But instead I chose to change the game plan and knew if I was thoughtful enough I could prevent my children from being scarred for life by the whole experience of seeing what really goes on in an obstetrician's office.

Once in the examination room, we all played an exciting game called "turn around three times and count as many birds on the wall facing away from mommy as you can!" Do that until you hear the doctor say to mommy, "okay you can slide on up." The turning around three times part was incorporated in as a means to disorient them a bit to buy me more privacy time. Whoever counted the most birds won! Guess what? Everyone won. It was all good. As a matter of fact, subsequent conversations about our family and the baby became more meaningful with more excitement after our trip to the doctor that day.

Children are natural-born truth seekers and totally see through the facade of parents who are disengaged. Parenting is a job that calls for coming to grips with parental responsibility along with great insight and lots of fun rolled up into as many experiences as possible.

People need to make the commitment to parent properly the moment they are blessed with this role. The wills and beliefs of parents will be validated some days and on other days totally crushed, dependent upon the experiences. That is part of the wonderful journey toward enlightenment.

Children simply help people evolve faster with the lessons they teach. Lighten up and sustain a place in your heart of acceptance and love so you can continue to be gentle with yourself and your child as you both grow and learn. Parents who truly get to know their children for who they were born to be understand the rhyme and rhythm of parenthood, making interactions full of more delights than struggles. Tasks at Hand can help elevate awareness, cultivate joy, and deepen relationships among parents and children, especially during times of simply being present together.

LIFE LESSONS

The final component in *Build Your Village* has to do with welcoming all *Life Lessons* and special teachers of life. Sometimes they come at the most capricious of times and in the darnedest of ways. A Buddhist saying is, "when the student is ready the teacher appears." That is to say, if you keep your eyes and hearts wide open you can learn so much from those around, especially children. Teachers in school play a very significant role, but even more important is the consideration of those real life experiences with people who pass through life and unexpectedly teach essential *Life Lessons*.

While some encounters may feel thorny at first, these unique experiences may result in an exact moment of enlightenment. We are all learners and, amazingly, all teachers as well. This means we travel through life teaching and learning in all directions with lots of different people. Remain open to those opportunities. Tremendous possibilities for growth exist when children are stimulated by things that appeal to their curiosity. Consider the value of unintended increase of awareness from people who pass through life. *Life Lessons* touch you, teach you, and significantly impact your journey.

The teachers I wish I had growing up are not necessarily the people best suited to teach my children. Everyone has his or her own style of learning and way of connecting. A good teacher provides the encouragement and guidance a child needs to believe in themselves that can ultimately change their life path. Every child needs a person they can trust and go to when they need help. Parents want it to be them, but in reality they need to realize that children may feel more comfortable with another person, family friend, teacher, or neighbor.

The people children are drawn to are often the ideal teachers for their present needs. Notice the people they are attracted to. Often they are good teachers for their current life studies. Welcoming *Life Lessons* means letting go of the ego and being available for your child while simultaneously allowing others to share their knowledge with them. *Life Lessons* come in a variety of packages. One may even be a person you may not particularly care for. That may be a specific time when the message being taught is just for you. The moment you open your mind and heart and can find an appreciation of something greater than your self is precisely when the *Life Lesson* is learned.

I have been fortunate to have many teachers show up throughout my life in the form of friends, neighbors, relatives, teachers, and even my grade school crossing guard. I have been taught awesome lessons of love that were so influential in shifting my understanding of humanity and the world at large.

I am so grateful for the lessons I learned from every single person I've met. *Life Lessons* can be discovered through a challenging event or a wonderful experience, either way they are gifts to encourage individual development. I try to share as many *Life Lessons* of my own with my children so that they see the variety and influence that any experience can have on a person's life. No matter how young or old, how long we spend with a person, or the title of the relationship memorable moments from lessons learned are carried for a lifetime in people's hearts.

Parents who make concerted efforts in combining the best people, environments, tasks at hand, cultures, and life lessons support their intentions of raising an amazing generation of smart, compassionate, successful children. Parents influence their children's lives more than anyone. In a world that may seem negative and full of challenges, it becomes vital for families to strike a balance with the perfect blend of elements for their personal villages.

Build Your Village allows parents to set themselves up for reaching a higher realm in peace and harmony regardless of what exists in the outside world. Those circles of influence can be the catalyst for true awakening and freedom from negative thinking. In an effort to raise the standards of parenting, let us work toward building harmonious villages of love, kindness, and respect for ourselves, our children and, for the entire world.

Part Two

WING IT

Chapter 6

Welcome Children into the Process

Nothing good comes out of creating a space that you don't feel welcome in. Really great things come from happy, joyful places. You need a gentle, soft, fun place to work in, and wherever you can keep it light, you should.
- George Clooney -

Modern day parenting requires a whole new perspective. Children in today's world need to be part of the process. Any approach in parenting today involves a distinctive philosophical difference in order to succeed. There needs to be more of an independent shift from parents always saying "no" first and limiting children out of fear to parents developing faith in their child's ability to make decisions and handle things in real time. The only way to get there is to *Welcome Children into the Process* and practicing a genuine exchange of ideas as they journey through life experiences. It's not about saying 'yes' simply to be liberal and permissive but rather saying 'yes' with the confidence and willingness to provide guidance to children as they navigate their experiences.

Parenthood can easily plunge people into a deep state of fear. Yet, the fundamental philosophy behind this book can help parents learn to let go in an effort to help children to take root and cultivate their wings. There is value in the balance presented to children with experiences that naturally prepare them to reach their promise.

Relaxing the grip in parenting is not about neglecting responsibility but rather making life easier and more fulfilling. It's about responding to a confusing yet exciting period of time with a very open way of thinking, and an adaptable frame of mind that encourages true collaboration with children. This breakthrough type of thinking will reward individuals with greater joy and success in today's world.

Whenever children ask for something or are ready to try something new, parents need to remain objective. Keeping the communication unbiased, without leaning in one direction before a child has his or her chance to convey their perspective, provides the necessary space to develop intellectually, emotionally, and spiritually.

By carrying on conversations that are open and free, and not responding prematurely especially in a disapproving way, children learn to have faith in themselves and gain confidence. They become aware of how they can change their strategy when something is not working the way that they want it to and take accountability in their decisions. Parenting that is based on faith in the human potential is about saying "no" as a last resort as opposed to saying "yes" as a last resort. This is how parents *Welcome Children into the Process* in a healthy way.

Asking lots of questions and allowing for open communication from as early as possible involves children and helps parents exercise this practice. When a child provides his or her answers, parents may be surprised to find out that they are the ones limiting their understanding. Their child may have a plan and see things differently than them that can ultimately result in a positive experience.

Welcoming them into the process is all about parents having faith in their intuition, and their children. It's about raising expectations without fear and pre-judgments. A shift in the whole parenting experience occurs simply by involving children in the why and how of their decisions. Parents, in return, naturally produce liberating feelings when they *Welcome Children into the Process.*

Children innately understand that that their parents are paying attention and caring when they practice welcoming them into the process. They innately sense that they are responsible and feel trusted. Children have to learn how to make choices at every stage and understand the consequences of their choices as they grow. Whenever a child does something remarkably mature, parents need to acknowledge them for their good decisions. They need to make a big deal out of the good and a small deal out of the bad. Children who get reinforced for making good choices then automatically want to make more good choices. *Wing It* parenting is all about raising expectations naturally and developing self-reliance at people's own pace.

Welcome Children into the Process entails some emotional adjustment and a significant focus on shifting energy into supporting independence. It is about fearing less and trusting more and letting go while still leading. *Welcome Children in the Process* shifts values naturally for each individual and creates a learning experience for everyone. It involves the transference from the parent being the sole governing power in a family to leading with insight while generously listening to different perspectives. Parents guide, children are engaged and taught responsibility, and everyone feels valued.

This single choice to *Welcome Children into the Process* can change the course of both the parent and child's life. Parenting, done right in today's world, includes the understanding that choice shapes the future. There must be a conscious release of past beliefs about authoritative-type parenting. Old school approaches do not work anymore because life is very different today.

Take a moment to imagine the kind of parent you wished you had growing up as a child. You may have wanted a parent who loved more and suffocated less, or a parent who supported and coached rather than yelled commands, someone who was more straightforward or kinder. Whatever traits come to mind, understand that you have the power to adopt those qualities as a parent yourself at this very moment. Together with your child, you can shape your life and make the choices that feel right for you both to help form wonderful life experiences.

You have the ability to change relationships within your family no matter the ages, past experiences, or present circumstances. Identifying personal hindrances will provide an opportunity to evaluate and begin the removal of doubt. Lessons in life prepare you for anything you want to accomplish. Once perspectives shift from life lessons, individuals can begin to feel less encumbered and freer to try their best. Gaining multiple perspectives is an impetus to growth and necessary to evolve, feel secure, and *Welcome Children into the Process.*

Clarifying a purpose by defining and shifting perspectives from that of powerless to empowered welcomes children and propels a more satisfying path of accepting and loving unconditionally. Healthy relationships help people identify who they were meant to be in this life so they can love without limits. Self-awareness helps people gain responsibility for understanding their own value and key influences, which ultimately facilitates uplifting and progressive action. It is only then that people can persevere with optimism.

Remaining self-focused helps people maintain peace and balance and provides a sense of ease and unwavering acceptance for children regardless of societal expectations. Staying self-focused gets easier as it's practiced. Taking care of myself helped me become a better person, which ultimately made me a better parent. This gave me the confidence to bring my children into the process without fearing the concept of losing control or losing my sanity.

Welcome Children into the Process is an ongoing undertaking. It refers to the conscious time and effort one takes to learn to trust their inner wisdom. Whether it is realized it or not, parents who wake up and evolve connect with their children in deeper ways. Parenting is an opportunity for parents to learn to appreciate the validity in the experiences of others without judging. No journey is better than another, just different, all of equal magnificence and importance. Children travel along their own paths as well. It is up to parents to accept that their children have their own journeys and remain generously supportive by leading them with faith and unconditional love.

It is an amazing opportunity to be a parent. It allows one the chance to raise awareness and inspire change in today's generation of children. People who are truthful in living life by remaining receptive to children's insight and ideas set positive examples for their children. Parents untethered by fears and misleading views have the greatest potential to unconditionally love their children. *Welcome Children into the Process* requires being comfortable with one self so genuine engagement can happen and children can grow well.

Be authentic and whenever questions arise, answer them honestly but appropriately. Parents need not lay personal fears or unsuitable problems on their children. Parents can be brave by admitting their feelings, faults, hopes, and successes but without burdening children with heavy, exaggerated emotions.

I remember when my daughter, then age six, noticed tears rolling down my cheek one day and stared at me in awe. She asked if I was crying. I hesitated for a moment. I was hurting and immediately wanted to screen her from my sadness. But, at that very moment I also realized I had only shared the strong, able-to-do-it-all mother and forgot to show her a more sensitive side. This one-sided image prevented her from knowing the magnitude of my personal makeup. The moment I shifted my external persona but not screening my emotions, I allowed my children to see all of me - the whole me. An authentic balance of emotions - minus the drama, helps children understand life better.

Many adults in our world have difficulty respecting children as they do adults. They assume because they are smaller physically that they are less intelligent or not as capable of making good choices. People who refrain from stifling their children or speaking for them show appreciation for their presence. They organically allow their children to learn responsibility without losing their handle on being a guiding force. Parents who practice being courageously welcoming to their children by taking a path of cooperation and respect rather than one of disregard and overpowering will have more a joyful and fulfilling parenthood experience.

One evening as my children, husband, and I were eating dinner, I read aloud a round table question I had cut out of a magazine earlier that day. It asked, *"What can you do better than your parents?"* My oldest daughter said without hesitation, she could ride horses better than us. That is the truth. My oldest son shared that he, in fact, knew all the Pokémon characters and my second daughter said she was able to twist her body up into a pretzel. This conversation starter took all of them all about five seconds to figure out what they wanted to say except for my youngest son who pondered the question for a couple of minutes and when everyone else had finished sharing he told us what he could do better than his parents.

At the ripe old age of four he valiantly turned toward my husband and me, looked us straight in the eyes and said, "I know how to LOVE better." The purity of those very words at that moment caused the hairs on my body to rise. Miraculously, the table was silenced by the comment he made, a mighty moment of honesty and love through the eyes of a four year old. He indeed continues to teach us every day how to love better. Sometimes too much, like when he invites the Chinese food deliveryman to have a sleep over at our house every time he delivers food. Nonetheless, he is an open, heart-driven human spirit who loves people willfully for who they are. I could not make him be like that. He simply is.

Without fail, whenever I *Welcome Children into the Process* I learn so much. As a parent, you are your child's first and most influential teacher. Being aware that they, too, are your teachers plays a monumental role in how one approaches parenting. By teaching them life skills, such as respecting others by respecting yourself, holding courageous conversations with them, and a willingness to include them in their development creates a profound impact. Children deserve sincere engagement and guidance with little interference from parents. Remaining aware of how powerful the influence of adults to children is along with understanding that children are stunted by any pushes towards forged ideas helps ease up the difficulty of parenthood.

Be observant of the dynamics created in their lives and use those moments to begin meaningful conversations with them, to encourage connections in order to understand life. A individual's potential to expand is illuminated through brave dialogues and explorations within their environment, by being involved and doing. Teach kindness, empathy, cooperation, consciousness, and appreciation by modeling that in your life. Everyone benefits when there exists a welcoming environment. It's becomes a win-win setting for life. When routines are created together and decisions involve all participants, every one inevitably takes responsibility. Essentially, a win-win translates to love and unity in relationships.

Being proactive by setting clear, age-appropriate, high expectations where achievement is easily recognized in an engaging way works to everyone's benefit. When conflicts arise, coming together with children to find solutions that are constructive creates a more harmonious climate, and willingness toward cooperation. Consciously staying mindful of the lessons children teach creates natural opportunities to evolve. Parents who remain kind and confident with their children hold a safe space for their personal evolution.

The beauty of participating in continual honest welcoming of children into the process creates more synchronization in family life. Just as with all organizations, success happens when the team has a unified vision and puts in a combined effort. Families also require an understanding that there exists flexibility in everything. Those who share open-mindedness and the consideration and appreciation of all members are successful.

Parental decisions in collaboration with a child's participation leads to the well being of the whole family. It is more loving to teach children to honor themselves, than always trying to do everything for them, which tends to slowly extinguish their self-confidence and development. The practice of including children in the process undoubtedly lessens stress and provides parents more influence. Consequently, life with children is made easier and more joyful.

Chapter 7

Intuit your success

There are so many paradoxes in parenting. But, hear wisdom's quiet voice and make it your own. Find strength in softness, power in flexibility, perfection in mistakes, success in failure, clarity in confusion, and love in letting go. - From The Parent's Tao Te Ching

To insist that there is a one-size fits-all model, and that there is one "right" way of getting to the finish line of success for parents is absurd. That is why parenting trends generate conflicts and criticisms. Parents know their children best. Bravely shifting from fear to empowerment by embodying what you believe in will consciously create a more authentic approach in parenthood and a life that is right for you and your children.

Parents these days have allowed the noise of others' opinions to drown out their personal wisdom and question their intentions. *Intuit your Success* is when parents can consciously pave their own paths by strengthening the influence of personal insight, opposing outside influences, and progressing freely toward what is right for them.

How does one intuit their success? By working it like a muscle -naturally. The most valuable tool available to people is their inner compass, their personal intuition. Every single person has this ability to sense it and utilize it. Intuition is custom-made for each individual. In all opportunities, it is a person's approach, their will to change, and their capacity to listen completely that determines the tone and outcome of those opportunities. Parents can intuit their own success by relaxing their grip on unconstructive ideas, learning to let go of what others say, and responding to their personal challenges by following their personal insight.

Humans have great power. As soulful beings, people are consistently being guided to be their best selves, if only they pause to listen. Intuition is that inner voice that speaks to you personally, regardless of what is happening with anyone else. The more you practice, the better you will get at understanding what it is telling you. The problem remains that most humans exist in a hectic world, making the ability to tap into personal guidance difficult, but definitely doable.

Being a good parent takes time to help constantly gain fresh perspectives, and to understand that even failures can be perceived as successes. Every person is the architect of their life and has the power to change only him or herself. It's how individuals approach experiences that teach valuable life lessons. The goal of reaching a personal unwavering capacity to love and appreciate oneself will set into motion the gift to love children for who they were born to be and the paths they are here to take. People need to love more and think less. Those who love themselves have an easier time creating personal balance and grasp the value of *Intuit Your Success*. Parents who allow others to influence their decisions need to seriously reflect on the responsibility of raising their own children and what that means.

The sense of intuition awakens when the mind is free of all concerns. Basically, when you are still, daydreaming, or even exercising your mind pauses and you become more attuned to your intuitive voice. Intuition comes from freedom, faith, and the understanding that each person comes to this earth with a unique purpose that is far greater than ever imagined. Parents have the responsibility to parent from the heart regardless of warnings and advice from the external world. Use your best judgment and you won't go wrong.

By calling on one's inner wisdom, and making choices from the inside out, people foster connections and ideas that lead gracefully to success. Intuition is like an inner-body compass that tunes into a person's thoughts and aspirations to steer them in the perfect direction. It is a subtle, yet complex threading of knowing that outperforms intellect any day. The force of fundamental truth or intuition is within all humans, no matter the age or experience. The ability to tune into it is dependent on how much an individual tunes in to it and uses it.

Children have far more wisdom and abilities than imagined because they are connected to their intuition more so than adults. Grown-ups tend to ignore their internal perceptions and permit outside exchanges of information to lead them astray. Also, adults often have layers of emotional baggage that hinder their ability to trust in their wisdom. Intuition is that gut feeling of knowing. It is more than an instinct. There is a definitive significance when people sense their intuition. It's when no one can convince you otherwise about what you know is true. Connecting with those thoughts regularly leads individuals to intuit their success. The more one practices listening to their intuition, the more it will develop. The all-inclusive intelligence of insight helps guide people through life and, when used by parents, it teaches their children to value their own intuition.

Parents step into their brilliance when they trust their insight. Applying these natural-given perceptions in experiences with children teaches them to listen and trust their intuition as well, a priceless life lesson. The more people unify the messages from their minds, hearts, and intuition, the easier life becomes. *Wing It!* parenting is all about connecting with faith and using intuition to ease up and live happier.

People reach success with the blending of heart, mind, and intuitive wisdom. Observe how a child naturally communicates what is in their heart and on their mind. It comes easily to them. They know which way they want to go. If parents allow children that independence, they will see that they know, more often than not, what they naturally need. Whether it is a child who likes to graze all day long rather than eat three meals a day, or the one who automatically reaches for a person who is really fun to be around rather than someone who is tense. They know. They use their intuition. It's adults who teach them to stray from trusting that well of knowledge. People need to recognize and believe in its brilliance.

Intuit Your Success involves the connection of mind intellect and heart wisdom, which is true KNOWing. It is about developing a whole new vision of living without needing to ask others their opinion. The connection between heart and mind encourages peaceful actions, and a knowing that helps people feel more secure. It's the easier way to navigate life during these quickly changing times. Stimulating intuition promotes accuracy in decision-making and goal setting. Our world is so rapidly evolving and parents who gain clarity about using their intuition will make room for new perceptions to emerge. Remaining adamant about one idea or approach hinders a person's ability to hear their intuition. In an ever-changing environment, it is about listening to personal wisdom and living openly to the joy life for healthy development and success.

The traits one is born with along with the environment they live in and the cultures they are exposed to, all together determine their success in life. How individuals define success is subjective and continues to produce more assorted variations today than ever. People have many possibilities; even those children who do not have their genius acknowledged in childhood or feature a breakaway talent. How a child is raised influences them to become the people they are. If they are raised in a controlling, heavy-handed manner they will lose sight of who they are and what they can offer the world. However, if they are raised in an unhurried pace and intuitively, they will be able to find their purpose magnificently as they mature. And those individuals who discover their intuition reach success confidently.

Listening to the wisdom of one's heart or intuition is a challenge for those who grew up valuing intellect. But it can be developed through the practice of acknowledging the abundance of insight each person holds. Intuition leads people to their limitless potential and in a direction that is best for each individual. Everyone can strive for success and all can attain it at their own pace and on their own terms. Parents should seek elements within their children that spark their passion and their abilities, and should thus remain supportive for in every human's core there exists the promise to succeed.

Intuitively, as parents we know who our children are. They show us at very early stages if they are adventurous or artistic, builders or problem solvers, settlers or dreamers, whatever they are makes them creatively unique. Whatever traits they demonstrate, intuition can help nurture their gifts. With little interference from parents, children can grow to be the best they can be. Yet, we often mix fear into the equation and conceptualize the worst-case scenarios rather than looking at the best outcomes that involve those characteristics. Parents who remain uncluttered and focused on what is right in front of them, without prematurely worrying, will be guided properly in all circumstances

Often, people exhibit a need to search a deeper intuitive awareness in the wake of challenging situations, when the intellect cannot comprehend difficult events. That is when people try to grasp an understanding from deep within their being. In order to gain comprehension, people look inward during complex periods to obtain some meaning or hope.

Individuals can become enlightened by simply co-creating things desired absent of fear, and not necessarily waiting for a trial in life to compel them to shift perspectives. The intention to evolve without needing challenges promotes an uncomplicated awareness and is the first step in being able to *Intuit your Success*. When a person lets his or her mind and eagerness quiet down before they make decisions, they are being prudent in listening to their intuition. Life, then naturally becomes easier because they are following a loving and authentic path.

If all people learned to listen to their intuition, the world would be a very different place. Humans actually gain energy when they do something intuitively because it genuinely feels right and, deep down, are reconnecting to their souls. They instinctively know it's the right thing. Winging it is about consciously raising children and proceeding intuitively without the influence of fear. The strength of spirit unites with personal knowledge to support individuals in making the best decisions without worry. It ultimately enhances the journey with children by living with lots of conviction of what is advantageous for each person.

Humans are designed to be intuitive. Reaching balance physically, emotionally, intellectually, and spiritually works hand-in-hand with honing in on intuitive knowledge. All it takes is the willingness to trust and the intention to be open to all possibilities. This may not be easy at first because many societies, cultures, and families teach us to fear and follow. But trust that it can be done successfully. The choices parents make to trust and intuit brilliantly create the life they desire.

Intuit Your Success is about tapping into personal guidance that disarms fears and generates loving knowledge to use in whatever path is chosen. The most important first step people can take every day is to tune into the voice of intuition that is filled with optimism and faith. The practice of using intuition in the moment-to-moment decisions will reap unprecedented rewards that allow parents to be successful through complex times. Taking steps to live intuitively is a new way to experience parenthood and certainly a great way to reach success with today's generation of children.

Chapter 8

NAVIGATE THEIR LIFE-EDUCATION

Love of knowledge echoes in our hearts and nourishes great thoughts.   - Socrates

We know knowledge is power. Understanding what comes naturally to children and what makes them feel alive, and captures their imagination is vital in learning to be responsive and raise them successfully. Recognizing their strengths as early on as possible is a huge advantage. That way, parents can build on those qualities to create platforms for discovery throughout their lives. By enhancing children's strengths rather than trying to crutch their weaknesses, moves them smoothly in their desired direction and most importantly, allows them and their parents to have fun in the process.

Today's parents have a very important responsibility in regards to raising well-rounded children. To attain greater meaning out of life-education and navigate a course that is right for them, parents can hold safe spaces for their children to find their own way in the world by creating organic growth in order to form better connections to others, and to the greater world. Parents and children need to create achievable goals together. To *Navigate their Life-Education* means parents can provide children with experiences that are engaging, and interest their children while they hold people accountable, and remain responsible themselves in an unforced way.

There should be trust in the learning environments a child is placed in along with an understanding that cultivating their mind, body, and spirit takes a team effort. Parents need to design experiences that connect children to the real world and lessons should share messages of love and promise. Parents are responsible for navigating a child's life experiences by creating proactive circumstances, rather than reactive responses. Just like in a child's overall being, the focus needs to be on wellness, not purely remedying avoidable illnesses.

Life-education encompasses all that we present to children in an effort for them to develop intellectually, physically, spiritually, and emotionally. Parents need to be involved and take responsibility for guiding their child's overall learning experiences. This is why the significance of building a supportive village was presented earlier in this book. The powerfulness of a child's entire environment is why we must also hold places of learning accountable for what they offer. Sending your child to school or writing a check isn't good enough. Relying on the notion that if you pay for your child's education whether via school taxes or tuition will guarantee your child a solid educational experience is completely a copout. We all slip-up as parents, but this something that can be prevented and crafted to make it right for each individual child. Parents who are organized, involved, and thoughtful about the places of learning their children attend provide inspired opportunities for them.

Schools play a significant role in helping children grow. Unfortunately, there exist vast imbalances in schools across the nation and the world. Some schools are failing our children while others break down barriers and lift children up to reach their highest potential. Schools have the capacity to be spheres of hope or zones of despondency.

What is happening in some schools across the nation is immoral and inexcusable. But, on the other hand it is heartwarming to observe successful schools in action and how magnificently star teachers impact the lives of children. The divergence is wicked.

Overall, most schools have lost the capacity to change with the times and needs of the modern day child. One thing rings true, many schools throughout the world are driven by fear, focus too much on one type of development, and assess children unfairly. Children and teachers are ruled in or out by grades and data rather than supporting individual strengths. Somehow, the entire system has forgotten the importance of understanding people from the inside out, honoring children for the unique beings they are, and preparing them for life in the real world where anything is possible.

What should parents ask of their schools? There needs to be a more loving, well-rounded focus on the whole child. Parents need to pay attention and teachers need more support. A great teacher is priceless and makes excellence in education possible.

Parents who sit idle or in silence are being unproductive and irresponsible. It is time parents and educators alike become the game-changers this unique generation of children is dependent on. When parents and teachers collaborate, children flourish. *Navigate their Life-Education* is about parents genuinely honoring their children and choosing programs and schools that support their beliefs and help children discover their potential.

Schools encourage intense academic competitiveness and often value one type of success based on generic formulated standards. Parents are compelled to act with a sense of urgency in response to out-dated environments and the disconnection in relationships some children experience when they attend school.

There exists a lack of consciousness. We need revolutionary ideas and actions now. Bullying is at an all time high. Ironically, character education programs are put in place as separate entities instead of being woven into the tapestry of school culture, and lived every moment. Children are screaming out for some recognition, validation, and help in making sense of this disconnected system.

Schools must focus on overall development and wellness as they value diversity and progress of today's children. America's educational system was established in the nineteenth century to meet the needs of a very different era. Schools were formed in order to teach people to assemble and manufacture things quickly for the industrial age. The goal was to be able to complete a set of predetermined tasks to get to the end result. At this moment in time, we need to radically rethink and restructure the educational system to meet the needs of independent creators, thinkers, and doers of today's generation.

Now is a time when intellect and innovation need to merge to create a diverse, dynamic, and interactive new presence, and sustain a world that learns from leaders from all arenas not just those limited by politics and religion. It is a new generation and the perfect time to promote learning from doing, exploring, and discovering independently.

Schools that foster a sense of purpose for today's children support their full development. If that does not exist, then parents need to supplement meaningful experiences for their children. Parents ought to promote opportunities for children to develop by honoring their individual uniqueness. They can respond to children's interests and curiosities with open-mindedness and global perspectives. Parents who understand the importance of embracing diversity, play, discovery, and innovation beyond the early years will raise children who can think for themselves, and mature completely in intellectual, physical, spiritual and emotional ways. Parents can be the catalysts for making their own child's life-education largely fun, culturally significant, and deferentially purposeful – without over-scheduling or overwhelming them.

Navigate their Life-Education is about finding the most meaningful opportunities for each child, independent of what their peers are doing. When lessons have significance and goals are individualized to meet the needs of a child they will spark excitement and interest in an organic way.

Today's parents are critical components in the process, and as such will help children tremendously when they remain mindful throughout their experiences. Opportunities offered both in and out of school should be supportive of individual strengths. Making meaningful connections prepares children for real life. If our educational system dwelled in the souls of children and assessed them for kindness, love, and understanding, our nation would be very different. Parents and teachers alike who teach children empathy, values, and acceptance as they build healthy bridges of understanding and trust in relationships inspire children's life-education experiences.

People who go beyond managing behavior, controlling, and being reaction-based to knowingly creating collaborative learning cultures for children serve their purpose and magnetize happiness. Being conscious of a child's life-education includes encouraging them to form self-built bridges of understanding so they can be their best selves.

Navigate their Life-Education is about investing in the construction of genuine relationships that help teach children about life. There needs to be an emphasis in understanding multiple perspectives and soulful solutions so children can prosper in today's global world. Having respect as a central theme in today's parenting involves a sincere belief that each child is valued and encouraged to grow independently.

In every facet of life, growing resilient to outside influences and tapping into personal wisdom allows people to walk a more authentic path. *Navigate their Life-Education* is not an attempt to get into the perfect school or have your child become an accomplished prodigy by age five, but rather a devoted endeavor to help them learn and grow lovingly in order to strive towards fulfillment. In the central mission of synchronizing life, it is about individualizing a child's learning experiences so they can feel successful. It is a confidence in knowing who your child is tempered by the humility in appreciating who they will grow to become.

Parents who personalize and remain reflective in regards to their child's life-education make the most out of life experiences, rather than following defunct systems and ideas that so often hinder happiness. They have a firm grip on the pulse of their child's potential, and help cultivate them into whoever they desire to be. A concerted effort in the ideas behind navigating life-education means allowing children to build their own courage, character, and confidence the way that feels authentic to them.

> "The child with his sweet pranks, the fool of his senses, commanded by every sight and sound, without any power to compare and rank his sensations, abandoned to a whistle or a painted chip, to a lead dragoon, or a gingerbread dog, individualizing everything, generalizing nothing, delighted with every new thing, lies down at night overpowered by the fatigue, which this day of continual pretty madness has incurred. But Nature has answered her purpose with the curly, dimpled lunatic. She has tasked every faculty, and has secured the symmetrical growth of the bodily frame, by all these attitudes and exertions—an end of the first importance, which could not be trusted to any care less perfect than her own."
> Ralph Waldo Emerson

Society, beginning at the earliest stages, bombards parents with methods claiming to help improve knowledge and skills to get children ahead. And because of that academic achievement is in the forefront of concern for most parents today. So, even though people continue to advance in most areas, there exists a lack of synthesis in the way we support humanity's progress. People continue to place such an important value on intellectual advancement. In many ways, people's thoughts are stifling their improvement as parents. Once people realize the importance of changing their thinking, they will lead far happier lives. Values resonate differently with each human being. Therefore, what you believe in guides your life and who you become. Parents have the opportunity to shape strong foundations for their children as they invest in what matters, get rid of excess, and navigate their life-education.

People who use intellect to discourage connection of heart and soul will continue to cling strongly to academic processes and outcomes. Things that settle in the brain but forget to consult with heart wisdom, and intuition result in premature execution of a task rather than expansion of the spirit. Parents of today must support all aspects of human development in order to help this generation of children succeed. We have already established that all children are each born with unique gifts. Gifts, that more often than not, go unnoticed because they don't necessarily fit into society's defunct or preconceived ideas of success.

Any personal attention parents give to *Navigate their Life-Education* influences the strength of their children's foundations and directly speaks to how they value individualized potential. The alchemy of all components, mind, body, and spirit, rests in the hands of adults who can inspire children, discover their specialness, and support their individual growth by empowering them. Modern day life-education requires true engagement that leans favorably to those who remain open to a life designed with hope and purpose so that children can soar.

Chapter 9

GET REAL SIMPLE

If you want to be happy, set a goal that commands your thoughts, liberates your energy, and inspires your hopes.
- Andrew Carnegie -

Get Real Simple is about de-cluttering your life and that of your child's so living becomes easier. Life today is complicated enough. The world is ever changing and continually evolves in a stronger, more complex, and faster way. Often people are absorbed in a focus of maintaining a certain status not necessarily matching individual purposes. Attention to goals that are unauthentic makes life even more complicated for families who then become burdened by floundering ideals and unnecessary excessiveness. People who are engrossed in keeping up with what they suppose to be the "best" are less invested in being present and enjoying real life.

Today's generation of children is so developmentally advanced physically, intellectually, spiritually, and emotionally that they naturally thirst for environments that are grounding and inspiring. In order to support them in their growth, parents need to simplify modern day life. The focus needs to be on intentionally designing family life to be the nuclei of composure and peace, tailored to be supportive of balance and individual purposes. That way, the chaotic issues that infiltrate the world at large, will not affect their personal spirits or diverge them from their aspirations.

Parents who understand their child's preferences and needs – not wants, will move along easier and *Get Real Simple* in their understanding of how to progress in life happily. As a result, there will be more allowing and appreciating what exists without the need to force or control things. The concept of allowing is not an easy task. Most everything our culture preaches has to do with working hard to get where you want to go. But, there is another way of believing, that is, to set yourself up to allow. Allowing and supporting individualistic family-friendly environments where there is trust and faith will simply make life more enjoyable.

Taking on the responsibility to do everything for everyone and trying to reach specific external levels that are forged, create more complicated lives. Parents who practice approaches that are controlling and are underlined with fear, will continue to create difficult experiences for themselves and their families. However, those who find personal satisfaction in a life that makes sense for them and their families by making the day-to-day happenings personalized and uncomplicated will establish conditions that bring about innate perspectives that positively work to their advantage.

With each person's culture, and the enormous collection of societal rules that come with the role of parenthood, and all the responsibilities present in today's world, solutions have to be unique and personal. Success occurs when people have high, self-created expectations that transition life into moving fluidly and reaching fulfillment. Being bombarded by other's attitudes and must haves only hinder the approach for parents to *Get Real Simple*.

Get Real Simple is a way of thinking, an aspiration, and a life choice. People who sift through life options and choose ones that make living less constricting naturally teach their children to support their individual potential. *Get Real Simple* is about creating ample space in life for the things one desires, and letting go of things that bind them or prevent them from moving towards personal fulfillment.

Get Real Simple is so necessary in today's complex and stress-filled environment. It eliminates old thinking and cultivates new practices that encourage parents to pause so they can help children create organic life courses that recognize their uniqueness. Parents need to take a leap into minimalism, that is, a life responsive to opportunities in a simple, smart, and unfussy style.

A world that feels chaotic, hurried, and materialistic often focuses on an excessive collection of stuff. Even before a baby is born, the pressure of buying all the baby stuff is enormous. The consumer market is massive, and the pressure for parents to fill their environments with gadgets has become tremendous. Getting caught up in this frenzy of filling life up with materialistic stuff promotes a more complicated existence and often hinders happiness.

Get Real Simple is a reminder to take this moment in time and surround your self, and your family with the easy, uncomplicated things that you love and makes you happy. It's the moment-to-moment experiences of joy that are remembered not the amount of things collected. Children living in a complex world deserve simplicity.

Children are born natural seekers. They orbit around their parents, observing and taking in the how and why people live the way they do. They do not respond to words as much as they react to what is being demonstrated. They feel the angst from those who make life harder than necessary. Parents who are confident and find their own balance naturally engender trust and confidence in their children.

Think about the simpler times from your childhood. What is cherished the most are the feelings and connections with people, not the stuff. By noticing when your heart sparkled as a young child can bring about powerful reminder of what's really important. *Get Real Simple* pays homage to the times when life was less complicated and people enjoyed life. This lifestyle is up for anyone to get a hold of. All people have to do is begin to slowly weed out the chaos and fastidious situations that take them away from truly loving life.

Parenthood is no time to put more pressure on one self, rather a time to create environments that are more loving, welcoming, and trouble-free. Elements from the outside world, which are unsupportive of a person's purpose, make life more complicated and messy. Pretending to live authentically clouds happiness, squashes dreams, and hinders an ability to live openly while raising children. But, within each home, parents can focus in on personal preferences and embrace meaningful opportunities and things that support their evolution.

As a little girl, I recognized the power of *Get Real Simple* with a story that is close to my heart and remains one of my favorite childhood memories. This memory that I am about to share has to do with my grandmother, my school crossing guard, and tomatoes; a true life lesson on how to *Get Real Simple* and enjoy the beauty of life.

A huge influence in my life growing up as a non-English speaking daughter of Greek immigrant parents was my elementary school crossing guard. Her name was Rosie. She was a salt-n-pepper haired, thick-boned, olive skinned, second-generation Italian-American woman of average height with whom I could never get my hands to touch when we hugged but, still holds one of the warmest places in my heart. I still remember the tone of her booming voice yelling at me for crossing in the middle of the street instead of at the corner.

I liked hearing her loud, raspy yells as she hollered at me because, in a strange way, it meant she cared. I remember her body warmth and the smell of her floral perfume when she wrapped her full arms around my boney-framed shoulders and walked with me, side by side, across the street to the corner where she happily sent me off to school. Those robust Rosie side hugs, even on days when they were wrapped in a yellow plastic raincoat, fueled me with love, and got me through the days when I often felt like an outsider. She exuded sincere love as she cared for the children she crossed every day.

Rosie was stationed at the corner of my large red brick, three-story childhood home. As unique as we were, she accepted and found a common thread of understanding with my family. Growing up in a very traditional Greek family in suburban Long Island back in the seventies was not easy. Most non-Greeks, including schoolteachers, did not quite know how to handle a little frizzy-haired, olive-skinned, skinny girl who could not speak much English. But Rosie was different than other people. She often took care of my favorite baby doll for me while I went to school and looked me in the eyes as she spoke to me. She respected my entire family. She took the time to listen to everyone in my family without judgment.

Rosie shared a special relationship with my yiayia, who now at age 101 still speaks about five words in English. They shared a mutual respect for each other that was tangible. The appreciation of one another's willingness to listen and graciously communicate without fear of being misunderstood, along with pure humanity was highlighted in every interaction they had. The simple fact that they did not speak each other's language was no excuse for avoidance. Quite the contrary, the love and respect I witnessed as a child is engrained in my childhood memories.

It was common to see Rosie leaning on one side of the chain-link fence that surrounded our property as she waited for children to cross. Yiayia stood along the other side of the fence passionately discussing everything from the trials of life to the aggravating insects destroying her roses. Together, they spoke about the weather, their families, current events, and their worry for the children as cars drove rapidly past them. A conversation that stands out in my mind is one I heard while walking home for lunch one day. At first I thought it was about yiayia's tomatoes and garden but as I grew older and more enlightened, I appreciate the greater life lesson in that powerful exchange.

The year must have been around 1978 and planting season was slowing down when school began. Our entire side yard, which today is a simple grass covered plot of land that often accommodates my father's fishing boat or trailer, was then strictly designated for the family garden.

I still remember the repeated ticking sound of the sprinkler as it moved back and forth watering the large bustling garden every night throughout the summer. Weeding and picking ripe vegetables was a common past time for the family and had to be done whenever yiayia or my mom decided to slip on their gardening shoes and go in. Every night, right before dinner either one of my siblings or I had to collect the vegetables that were ready to be picked, being careful not to step on any good ones or grab anything rotten with our bare hands.

Summer had ended and we were into the first week of school when yiayia had spent an afternoon picking the select few vegetables that were remaining in the garden. She gathered a couple of peppers, a few cucumbers, and the last of the garden's lingering homegrown tomatoes. They were big and red with hints of green stripes, a few days from being really ripe and delicious. No doubt, in less than a week they would be perfect for a final yummy homemade summer salad.

I watched yiayia graciously put the other vegetables down on the edge of the driveway as she carefully held the tomatoes close to her chest being careful not to drop them. She walked down the driveway and then to the corner where she met Rosie who was standing there waiting to cross children. Yiayia handed the handful of tomatoes to Rosie and wished her good health and a safe new school year.

They reminisced about the circle of life and another summer coming to an end.

As yiayia walked away, she made the sign of the cross, as she often did to bless Rosie. She lifted her arms to the sky to thank God for the peaceful break Rosie got over the summer and then clutched her arms together over her heart to wish her patience and strength so that she could, once again, keep all the children in her care safe and sound.

Their nods and gestures were a loving interaction that was a powerful message about true generosity. I did not even have to hear the broken words or entire conversation. I understood they were communicating the ways people should, and accepting each other the ways people ought to do. Yiayia spoke but a few words of English, and Rosie spoke no Greek, yet they communicated better than most people do today. Rosie walked across the street to place the handful of tomatoes she received on the seat of her warm car. She would share them with her family and remain thankful for the person who lovingly grew them.

Their combined gestures of wholesome compassion taught me a powerful lesson I still carry with me to this day. There are more loving people in this world than not. There is more good in this world than not. And there are abundant opportunities in this world for adults to teach children respect for themselves and appreciation for their surroundings if they just ease up and enjoy the simplicity of life.

Life can be as simple or as complex as people choose. Parents who focus on uncomplicated structures and opportunities that provide breathing space and pauses take the pressure off living and are able to *Get Real Simple* and enjoy life with their children more. Parents today, more than ever, need to make efforts to convey loving concepts to their children regardless of the alarming stories that dominate the news in society or the fearful approaches other parents may use.

Being self-focused is principally considering personal needs. Everyone needs that. Remaining understanding of one's personal needs prevents resentment for continual sacrifice and insufficient focus on self. Getting real simple in my life personally meant letting go of people and situations that created stress and worries. I began to release any event or circumstance that swallowed up my spirit or was highly demanding.

Independently focusing on me meant slowly but steadily infusing substantial alone time into every day. This practice is something invaluable that everyone can give him or herself, not only to set a good example for children, but also to find personal peace. There are still days when I do not have enough time for myself, but never is there a day when I lose my purpose or myself.

People can practice three things to get to the point where they can eliminate pressures of life and *Get Real Simple*. I refer to it as my three Rs: Relax, Regroup, and Renewal. Relax is taking time and continual moments to slow down. Intellectual, spiritual, emotional, and physical pauses give people time to help understand their whole self more. Time to do what is desired is crucial, not selfish. Always giving without receiving is a sure course to unhappiness and discord.

Regroup is when people temporarily focus and freeze the disorder around them in order to gather thoughts and reframe goals so they can move closer towards their aspirations. Some people need to mark it on their calendars others practice it weekly. However it needs to get accomplished, to Regroup is a gift that keeps people on task and moving towards their purpose.

Lastly, Renewal invigorates people's spirits and reminds them of the possibilities. It is the moment when someone is able to be reflective on what they want out of life, assess how they are doing, and proceed by engaging fully in life in order to renew their spirit. These three steps of Relax, Regroup, and Renewal help people and children create paths that are useful and fulfilling.

It was just a couple of years ago when I heard back from my childhood crossing guard, Rosie after I sent her a heartfelt note expressing the impact she made in my life. In her letter, she shared her gratitude for her life experiences with the children she crossed, and those she raised. She was one of my greatest teachers. My earliest lessons of true humanity were learned from her, and are ones that I have kept in my heart throughout my life. They were simple acts of kindness, and yet examples of humanity that makes the world so much sweeter. My perspective of never feeling that I fit in, on top of growing up in a traditional Greek family that was, at times, narrow-minded, did not obstruct my insight that all of humanity is interconnected thanks to Rosie's example.

Rosie recently passed away, but the simplicity in the lessons about love she shared will surely live on. She was certainly one of my most powerful teachers in life, and for that I am grateful. The choice to be appreciative of the simple things in life and communicate that with children is the responsibility of each individual.

Life is chaotic enough and parents need to restore some simply sensibility in their lives with children if they are to enjoy the journey of parenthood and succeed. Each person has the potential to love and create amazing opportunities in the simplest of ways. Once people edit all the nonsense out of their lives and *Get Real Simple*, they can see the benefits of experiencing life in a clearer and easier style, which then impacts children in a wonderfully positive way.

Chapter 10

INSPIRE INDEPENDENCE

The more you are motivated by love, the more fearless and free your action will be. - *Dali Lama*

Do you know who you are enough to allow your child to become who they are? That is the vital question that guides today's parenting. Fundamentally, ideals are formulated and decisions are made about what is best for children based on how parents feel about themselves. This premise determines how much faith parents have in themselves, and how much independence children are given.

This is a vital step of giving children growing space while simultaneously moving into personal heart wisdom.

Think about what you specifically need so you can feel whole and make good choices for your child. It is based on the ability to recognize one self through positive light in relationship with the current moment.

If we want children to grow up to be independent, we must set the example of remaining true to ourselves as we strive toward fulfillment. Today's world demonstrates an insatiability of excess. Everything is boosted up; people's wants, schedules, appearances, and need for acceptance. People have become encumbered, more than ever, with a need of materialism in a quest to find some sort of happiness.

Humanity's compass towards the most important things in life has become distorted, and never has there been a greater negative consequence than today's generation of children. There is a great disconnect in the ability to build relationships among parents and children due to the focus of life outside themselves rather than looking deep within, and moving ahead on independent paths. A life based in love, creativity, and enthusiasm for evolvement means a person is listening to their intuition and is living consciously connected to the world around them.

Inspire Independence is all about how parents allow children to navigate through life and empower them with choices. It refers to the successful set up of whatever is provided in an effort to help children reach fulfillment. It's about living more relaxed while discovering courage, confidence, and character. It is a conscious practice of living a balanced life of mind, body and spirit. Parents have a distinct responsibility to provide opportunities for children to grow in every capacity, to teach children to think independently, and to love unconditionally.

Each human being has a choice of how they experience life. Physical handicaps are no harder or easier to hurdle than intellectual or emotional ones. That said, it is every person's individual responsibility to grow a new sense of self, strut his or her individual style, and overcome adversity for personal advancement.

Enlightened people rarely subscribe to fear-based ideas or play into the role of inferiority. They have no time for limitations based on other's beliefs. Independence is more about attitude than it is about ability. It is about a person's willingness to walk with resilience and persistence toward what feels right in their core, and carrying a balanced determination to be the best in whatever role they take on in life.

Independence provides an opportunity for individuals to step into their potential. It often guides people in a new way to march out of any past chaos and discover how to savor the present. That's what children do. They help adults relish in all the wonders of life in a slower pace with more open eyes.

Wherever, and whenever individuals are able to pause and breathe in all the beauty of whatever is right in front of them influences their independence. Children are very keen in their abilities to absorb authenticity. Children observe people. They understand relationships, and the unspoken language of pure emotions. Good parenting in today's world looks very different than in past generations and involves breakthrough thinking.

Inspire Independence is based on stimulating children personally with new purpose and passion. Individuals who set positive intentions will arrive at their ambitions accordingly. Reaching a higher realm as a human, at any age, is all about being true to one self, loving unconditionally, and creating joy. Every single person on earth deserves to have everything they want. There are no limits, only those that people place on themselves or those that parents place on children. Limiting beliefs harm people's spirits and impedes happiness. Unconstructive thoughts and behaviors hold people back from accomplishing potential goals.

Today's parents must allow more and restrict less. They need to think about the "why" behind decisions and beliefs rather than repeating patterns just because that's the way it's been. Denying children things under the guise of safeguarding them is not necessarily the wisest path. To talk the talk without paying attention to what is being modeled diminishes the power of a life lesson.

Children naturally hone in on people's actions more so than verbal explanations. When people are in a good, reflective space that is aligned with integrity, life somehow gets easier. Parents need to really think about why they say and do the things they do. It isn't about trying to prove someone's worth but rather to understand the reasoning behind what is best for each individual at that specific moment.

The quality of parent's ability to provide independence directly affects the quality of the soil that helps root their children in self worth. As each child assumes different responsibilities and experiences throughout life, they pick up tools, ideas, and other things that can accelerate or decelerate their growth.

Parents who *Inspire Independence* stimulate spirit consciousness, the discovery of personal talent and gifts, as well as wonderful experiences for all those that share in the journey. People who stay present in their own lives, and create their own joy, regardless of what happens around them are more successful. They are referred to as independent thinkers.

Parents can grow independent thinkers. To support their children in striving to be their best in whatever it is that they choose to pursue is always a choice. Choice is power, and empowerment naturally leads to independence. In today's global world this remains every parent's responsibility. Parents who allow the spirits of their children to shine through naturally *Inspire Independence.*

Navigating life based on influences outside one self, and not living authentically for personal fulfillment leads to personal conflict. External influences such as primary family experiences, media, religion, school systems, and societal expectations all play major roles in the ebb and flow of life. They also influence how parents raise their children.

Children of the past were often taught to ignore their inner knowledge of what was right for them and follow "in their parents' footsteps." "Old school" parenting had a different purpose and rhythm that does not work with today's generation. Children that were raised in a controlling or dependent way are now adults who have completely rebelled against their upbringing or are unable to take responsibility in life. Today, parents know better, and so there needs to be a major change in attitude.

Current parenting trends seem to have lost touch with the importance of healthy relationships and connections human beings need to grow and flourish in a world that is global. By simply recognizing the influences that sculpt individual journeys, and the importance for each child to be inspired to live independently by providing unconditional love and guidance, today's parents will create a more balanced, purposeful, responsible generation.

We all need to acknowledge that society categorizes people even in the earliest stages of human development. This makes walking independently in one's truth even more challenging. People are judged based on preconceived notions, external success markers, and fear-based life styles. The host of platforms that penetrate today's everyday life convey messages to people about how to "be a man," or "act like a lady," what they should say, how they should sit, what size bodies they should have, and how certain body parts should look. These super strong ideas influence an individual's sense of worth and how they exist in the world.

Parents need to be the antidote for these sometimes-destructive influences. Encouraging individuality and acceptance for each child can cure this problem over time. But, for now, parents who *Inspire Independence* are the pioneers who will shift mindsets of what good parenting looks like. Bravo to those who encourage their children to be proud of who they are and what they bring to the world, and honor their individual traits, ideas, and potential.

So, by this point you may be wondering... How did I get to this enlightened point of knowing how important it is for parents to *Inspire Independence*? I was forced to understand it personally. I had no other choice than to re-direct myself toward a healthier way of living by the time I had my second child. This is when I finally realized the importance of learning how to care for myself first, and teaching my children to be less dependent on me.

About six months after I had my second child I could not get out of bed. I felt exhausted and nauseated. My first thoughts were that I had to be pregnant but, it felt more arduous than that. After visiting my doctor and a slew of blood work, I was diagnosed with an autoimmune disease that went undiagnosed for years. It was like I was walking in darkness for months and found myself physically, spiritually, intellectually, and emotionally exhausted.

So, there I was, overwhelmed, frightened, and in a complete fog but had the main responsibility of being a full-time mom to two little girls. I was often jolted out of a daze with fictitious, panicked-ridden scenarios, and would go through my daily routine staggering erratically like a car running out of gas. I was being held down by the overbearing weights of parenting dictated by external societal expectations that caused unnecessary and unconstructive pressure. I had lost myself, yet I continued to dig my heels deeper into the "perfect" mother-wife-homemaker role.

Women usually fall into this trap more than men when they identify themselves so stalwartly in one specific role. My role was that of "do-it-all woman." It was a deep hole of failed expectations that created a vicious cycle of helplessness that I was only able to recognize as it manifested into an illness that knocked me out.

What I learned from that challenge is that there is no value in valiantly attempting to become the be-all-end-all person in a child's life. The role of a parent is about making connections with children while encouraging them to be all they can be independent of any one person. I was able to get myself out of the fog by focusing on me and understanding the importance of providing opportunities for my children to gain their own independence. The moment I understood that, I was on my way of feeling better and being better.

I had to break the unproductive pattern of trying to do it all for my family. After all, I felt I could do it all myself. What I did not realize at the time was that I was indeed doing it all, but not doing it all well. I needed "me time," and some help in order to enjoy the journey of parenthood.

People who pay attention to their personal needs are more content and able to share genuine love and consideration with others. A person's adventure in self-discovery, when observed by children, will actually cause them to rethink their own life paths in a positive way. Parents who do this teach their children that there are always choices. It is each human being's birthright to focus on love, health, and strength for themselves. People need to honor their own life path while they help shape their child's discovery of who they want to become.

A strong sense of self, a curiosity, and an excitement in life helps people make strides and progress. It is the ambition to awaken, and an individual essence that helps sketch dreams and provides faith, and strengthens every step taken. Souls elevate whenever people plug into their own power and live as independent thinkers. Just like with children, an irresistible enthusiasm will build and build as people live as they were born to be.

Every parent can parent successfully. People who are able to negate outside influences have an easier time as parents. A being who walks independently in confidence, relies on nature's law of harmony that all living things have a blessed opportunity to flourish. Authentic journeys are more influenced by the miraculous occasions parents spend present, the ones that often do not get recognized by the outside world. It is not about tallying trophies, or what is bragged about through conversations in social circles, but rather a unify experience shared between two souls.

Inspire Independence is when individuals recognize success in parenthood in the moments of being present. Parents need to lead independently as they parent at their own pace on their own terms. And those who create a life that makes sense for themselves and their children without feeling burdened are naturally inspirational.

I have learned that the means to empowerment for anyone is always within reach. We have to simply pause and mindfully embrace life. Parents desperately search outside themselves for the right tools to "fix" a defiant teenager or make three-year-old's temper tantrum dissolve when they should simply detach from external expectations. They can accomplish this by searching intuitively to observe what role they play in the situation. The tenderness of parenting from an open heart is the best way to connect and to figure out how to resolve issues.

We are all responsible for teaching each other. Frequently it's at the point of pure exhaustion or discouragement that a flicker of insight helps people figure out what is needed in a conflicting situation. Just like the times that children feel most unlovable are the points when they need love the most. Children arrive in this world as individual spirits who possess unique personalities, learning styles, and talents. Parents can help them discover all that they are, and teach them to live independently when they remain open and flexible.

Life is always evolving. Children are growing. Parents are learning. And that's why people need to remain fluid. Parents intuitively know this from experience. If parents want children to learn to care for themselves then they need to model valuing their own selves. Life is about self-discovery and advancement. More than that, it is about the staying power people have in a continuous evolution of roles acquired and roads taken. Modern day parents especially need to find a neutral and productive point between an independent and authoritarian style as they move through parenthood because extreme approaches don't work.

What do we know about children? Children are born beautiful souls deserving of love for whoever they were born to be. A parent's job is to gain direct insight into their child's spirit by accepting their significance, and staying engaged at all stages in life by helping them reach their potential. Parents need to help them build a foundation for natural growth so they can have a solid platform to grow.

By nature people are curious creatures, born eager and interested, and they need trust and freedom to flourish and grow. Children also want to figure things out on their own and crave life exploration. Even from the tiniest of tots who chant how they want to try something new, children repeatedly display their independence and inquisitiveness. At a very early age, children demonstrate their liberty in wanting to be their own person. Successful parents allow them the space and establish adaptable bonds so that children want to stay connected but do not feel needy. They raise them to be independent through considerate love. No matter how you slice it, while some parents would rather hold on to their children as long as they can, they are undeniably self-determined spirits. And just like all living things, they have the power to guide their own lives. They just need a little help getting there.

Parents do not own their children; they are simply passing through their lives, and must allow them to be the wonderful people they are meant to be, and honor their paths. Children need parents to guide them, have faith, and then get out of the way. They are deeply profound, every single one of them. They are not empty vessels that need to be filled, but require guidance and acknowledgment for their amazing spirits to have the freedom to expand. Parents need to honor and love them for their possibilities even if it's not common practice.

Loving them for who they were born to be helps prioritize a parent's ability to guide and inspire children along with providing an undeniable acceptance for who they are. All it takes is a shift in believing in one self and trusting in the belief that some how, some way, what is necessary will be provided.

Children are quite simple in what they want and need. Try spending a few minutes outside playing in the dirt, or climbing a tree, or being anywhere in nature with any child. Notice how their "wants" adjust after a few moments outside because they have everything the need right there in front of them. They innately sense what is really important, that is, enjoying life. The best playgrounds are the ones that nature organically assembles; the massive climbing trees, slippery snowy slopes, or storm-induced ponds. These are gifts of nature reminding us to play and enjoy life more.

It is just like when children get a break from their schedules. They naturally become creative, imaginative builders and thinkers who get lost in play. Children crave independence and simplicity in play and in life. And it's often easy to tell if an adult didn't have enough time to play as a child or wasn't inspired to be independent. The great philosopher Plato once said, "You can discover more about a person in an hour of play than in a year of conversation"... how true that is.

Parents need to become more open-minded and *Inspire Independence* in order to experience their child's fullness and life to it's greatest extent. They need to sit on the floor and play; play that takes them out of themselves, and permits them to enjoy things that are really important, staying relaxed and happy. Fun in life happens whenever there exists encouragement for everyone to stay true to his or her essence tempered by gentle guidance.

Every child has the potential to be self-reliant, empathetic, and independent; someone who can give of themselves fully to our wonderful world if their surrounding environment just slowed down a bit, and stopped anticipating what's next. There are parents who anguish over teaching toddlers to read, go to the potty, memorize facts, or push skills that they are not ready to experience. Time and energy is often wasted in anticipation for the next step, the next accomplishment. And more disturbing are approaches that repetitiously drill tasks regardless of a child's readiness. Remember, what works with one child will not necessarily work with another. Parents who put forth personalized consideration just as they do for others in their life, and relax in their outlook and anticipation of getting ahead will consciously create environments that are safe and nurturing with an absence of false premises and unrealistic expectations.

I am blessed with five children who have been the best teachers in my life. They stretch my mind so much that at times I feel like it will snap. But, they have broken me open to the wonders of life. They have unraveled my uptight grip on life and taught me to trust that all things are possible. Whenever I think something is not doable, they show me the possibilities.

Some people may say it is not practical to allow children to think big, but I believe no one has the right to put limits on other people's dreams or abilities - no matter their size. I engage in the spirits of my children. Even at the height of the emotionally charged, frenzied days, I reflect on both the brilliant moments and the humbling settings. These times are needed to expand and grow, moments to learn to love yourself and to unconditionally love those people in your life.

Once parents courageously look within they gain direct insight to the spirit of their children. Children come into our lives to teach us what we are unaware of, and what we need to learn, to expand our minds, and enlarge our hearts like no other experience on earth. Those fortunate enough to have an opportunity to be around children, even if for a short while, should lean in and surrender to the beauty of this progression.

While respecting the fact that every child is born with their individual spirits, parents do have the ability and responsibility to guide them. Parents receive an amazing opportunity in raising children and basically their job can be summed up to simply not screw them up.

Parents need to have faith, to launch children to be independent, limit direction, and harness their talents. They require attention and nurturing, but it is not a good use of anyone's energy to micromanage children. They have far more wisdom and abilities than people think, and are naturally destined to reach success, which is defined differently for everyone.

All children have the right to a life filled with hearty giggles, inventive play, and lots of love. Each stage in a child's life is both a gift and challenge for parents and children alike. Parents who provide ample space that allows children to let their minds and hearts wander, and trust in their innate sense of wonder as they explore and expand, encourage healthy development. Adults can empower children by allowing them to make decisions for themselves thereby gaining self-confidence, self-love, and appreciation for their own achievements, which ultimately fosters personal drive to reach fulfillment.

Life is more about following one's curiosity than learning what others are teaching. Humans are inquisitive and naturally know what they like. Children can benefit from being encouraged in a loving way to try new things so they expand their preferences. Parenthood is not about taking on the task of trying to control children's lives; that just feels like swimming against a fierce ocean current. It is about accepting the highs and lows of life that sometimes create intricacy and self-doubt, courage and validation but in the end, an elevated understanding as a parent.

The moment parents release their grip on children, and accept every moment as beneficial for progress, they are able to pursue any objective. It takes practice to streamline into an *Inspire Independence* mode. It's a new way of thinking. Reminding yourself of the saying "this too shall pass" helps remove the cloak of worry, and switches energy to that which one can feel is real.

It is much healthier to stop micromanaging a child's development, and integrate the practice of simply being content with what exists regardless of what other parents are doing. Being generous with acceptance, respect, guidance, and engagement will feel right and organic. A level of confidence will emerge as parents *Inspire Independence* and witness the positive effects. It will be during those autonomous moments that children will feel loved for who they were born to be and parents will craft soulful connections with them as they thrive independently.

Chapter 11

Teach & Engage

Children grow well when their parents are growing well. - Albert Einstein

Parents and children these days are busier than ever. A reaction to the demanding busy lifestyles has become over-scheduling and relentless scripting of a child's play or learning. The influence of their learning is determined by the diverse opportunities that are woven into a child's day-to-day engagement.

Parents have the opportunity to seek teachable moments that support children who have dreams, visions, and passions that will guide them to their potential. This engagement requires ongoing observation, reflection of purpose, and inspired action. To *Teach and Engage,* rather than command and veto, imbues the parenting process with faith and optimism. Parents who practice this have an easier time recognizing benefits to challenges that arise, discover life lessons, and dissolve issues that may burden others. Innovation is key in the learning and engaging of today's modern day generation.

There is a greater, wide-ranging, more accepting, and respectful way to raise the children of today. It's a matter of considerately recognizing their innermost spirits while simultaneously rejecting the need to satisfy others. A good idea is for parents to continually pay attention to their child's passion, or what turns them on to life, to keep the faith, and then get out of the way so they can learn. There is no room for other people's fears to influence how to raise today's generation of children. The world can be viewed with optimism or negativity depending on individual perspectives. People who honor their dreams and appreciate their journeys have more hopeful outlooks and positive experiences. It is about using integrity and authenticity in making tomorrow a success by honoring oneself and empowering children to do the same. Being real is the best way to teach. Parents who succeed trust themselves and their children as both teachers and learners.

People who own their own wisdom, the knowing of who they are and what they want out of life, have an awareness that leads them to evolve. This understanding drives people to better experiences, deeper relationships, exciting opportunities, and fulfillment. Even at this moment of unlimited information and sprouting trends, the wisest decisions are based upon entering a genuine realm of being authentically confident.

Once parents become self-aware, they can begin to accept the past and intuit limitless possibilities for their future. Acceptance is golden. The realization for individuals to understand the responsibility lies in shifting one self and no one else - not their children, not their parents, not their partners, not their friends. The agreement of just that alone removes the huge burden people tend to carry around throughout their lives. It comes down to learning, accepting, and appreciating what exists in life at this moment. Trust that whatever exists is because it is supposed to be there. There are no coincidences. Everything in life exists to teach something, thus accepting the lessons life provides is a beautiful way to *Teach and Engage.*

In present day living, it is more obvious than ever that everyone is a teacher, and everyone is a learner. Therefore, parents who remain open to learning from their children as they teach them will struggle less. The ideas behind *Teach and Engage* embrace offering choices, providing clarity of expectations, and inviting children to be part of the overall objective of raising children successfully in today's world.

This includes breaking down bigger tasks so not to overwhelm, and helping children gain a sense of accomplishment as parents create a sense of belonging with routines and fun gatherings. Life is about learning, creating, and loving. It is not about embarrassing, reprimanding, or isolating children in order to make them feel insignificant and inferior.

Those antiquated tactics are not going to get the results in the long run. Environments that snuff out a child's specialness produce children with low self-esteem, disharmony, and even lasting rebellion. Parents, who raise children by teaching and engaging them, naturally produce ripples of optimism in their life experiences. *Teach and Engage* is more of a soulful way of helping children feel powerful and important.

Edwidge Danticat once wrote, "To teach children, give them access to stories about their potential, their power, and ability to contribute to the world." As children's primary teachers, parents have the opportunity to launch independence as they raise children to discover their paths, let them experiment freely, remain observant as they grow, and not make assumptions.

Taking time to really understand the soul of a child will facilitate seeds of worthiness and help nourish their gifts. Children's spirits must be encouraged, and free of conformity or bias. A parent's job is to identify the vivacity, which is within every single child. It is then that parents can confidently share that wisdom with others who impact their child's learning, creating an environment that allows their child to flourish.

Children's bodies and minds need lots of space to grow. Their spirits need affirmation and autonomy to explore their capabilities, talents, and interests.

When unconditional love permeates meaningful relationships within their lives, people are deeply fueled with purpose, and whatever they need to prosper.

Today, parenting must encompass essential elements that reinforce the teachings of raising new standards. Based on an independent mindset, these elements of what should be, what is right for each family, and the endless possibilities of what can be respect the whole child and the learning process as an individualized experience. This way of thinking encourages a courageous presence and the persistence of free exploration, deeper knowing, and liberty from the past, more so than ever before.

Individuals reading this book may want to ask themselves, "How can I parent differently knowing what I know now?" As stated earlier in this book, communication is key. How one communicates the *Teach and Engage* strategy determines how a child will receive it. If it is conducted as a relentless task or an angst-filled chore the process and results will be restricted. Teachings are better learned from parents who release fears and boost confidence naturally through play and imagination.

As leaders for this new generation, parents today need to seek opportunities to heal, grow, and connect for themselves and their children. There are no books that explain the intricate dynamics of parenting and how to understand all the complex facets thrust upon people in today's times. What is crystal-clear is that parents can no longer use the controlling, rigid strategies of the past. They simply do not work for today's generation of children.

There are defining distinctions between parents who govern out of fear and use inappropriate techniques and what children of the modern world will respond and learn from. That is why the philosophy behind *Wing It* is individualized, and based in cooperative agreement which helps cultivate meaningful growth in children. Ongoing personal development and self-awareness are key components in bringing forth the intuitive opportunities for learning, expansion, and parenting approaches that work successfully.

Good teaching launches discovery at every age. Authentic engagement allows children to explore and discover who they are, leading them gracefully to a stronger sense of self. Children are born curious and want to figure things out for themselves. They have minds of their own, are capable learners, and are uniquely creative.

All too often parents start out speaking at their children or answering for them. This is not how people promote growth. Remaining flexible and trusting in the *Wing It* process supports individual creativity. *Teach and Engage* plays into that by continually providing a supportive environment that supports a child's interests and capabilities in order to help them discover his or her greatness. It guides parents in honoring their children and who they were born to be. By identifying a child's gifts and encouraging them to take risks in learning, parents grant them a path toward dignity without having them prove themselves continually, or remain fearful of possible danger.

To *Teach and Engage* can be a springboard to living courageously even when doubts come in to play. There will be moments of trepidation. However, using this strategy will showcase people's strengths and wisdom. Children who are taught teach others, and parents who genuinely engage acquire confirmation of what is valued.

Those who appreciate the process and outcomes of being engaged with children, naturally perpetuate an attitude of valuing children. There has never been a smarter or more amped up group of children willing to be fully challenged to develop their minds, bodies, and spirits more so than today's generation. People who seek to find an empowering approach are being shaken into wakefulness to become the parents they always knew they could be. They recognize the choices they have in front of them and find better designs for parenting. The *Teach and Engage* model intuitively requires trust that brings about a life desired with infinite possibilities.

Today, like never before there exists a cultural consciousness among humanity. That is, responsive social skills that people use to interact, persevere, and build relationships with each other. People have never been so busy, hurried and, so connected all at the same time. A contemporary social, emotional, and intellectual approach to how people are able to parent and teach is essential in the success of this generation.

A synchronization of personal space, gaining multiple perspectives, and walking independently as global citizens will cause a tremendous shift in the parenting landscape of today. Parents have an incredible opportunity to guide and teach children as they pass through their lives. As children grow, parents can modify their teachings, yet remain engaged so that they can grow progressively as they define their authentic selves. Wayne Dyer refers to it as "non-interference" in the raising of children.

At a very early age, children demonstrate their independence in wanting to be their own human beings, while parents often hold them down. Amazingly, children have the power to create successful lives with very little interference and the help of adults who are willing to remain supportive and loving in an easy style.

Teach and Engage is about appropriately interacting with children by:

- Differentiating life lessons and teachings
- Raising expectations
- Inspiring and cultivating creativity
- Valuing everyone's perspectives
- Embracing, engaging in, and promoting empowering opportunities

Excellence is never accidental. The intent behind *Teach and Engage* can help determine success. It encourages a sense of fulfillment, confidence, and ambition that cultivates accomplishment. It authentically relishes in the nuggets of wisdom individuals share and honors the talent or strength in each of us. The propensity of each person's individual willingness to learn, grow, and love throughout life is determined by the intentions behind *how* they engage.

Parents show respect by providing their full attention and letting children know that they have been heard and understood. They express themselves honestly, and explain their viewpoints thoroughly but briefly. Successful parents initiate multifaceted experiences, but do not feel pressure to agree or share fearful predictions. They ask more questions as they wade through challenges. That is the magic of crafting engaging opportunities - to connect, communicate, and grow love by evoking consciousness through meaningful interactions.

Through *Teach and Engage*, parents have the amazing opportunity of helping discover children's gifts and talents. It is not about making them fit into specific boxes for easy labeling, but about honoring who they are meant to be so they can be best at being themselves. Parents should never stop paying attention. Children of all ages experience all of the different feelings they want to share with those they trust and love. Life is all about discovery. Children need to be encouraged to explore, question, collaborate, play, experience, and challenge themselves as they build bridges of understanding.

Generation after generation has been conditioned to continually enhance the mind, and focus on becoming smarter than previous groups. Often, people roam the earth in an intellectual, cerebral manner detached from their hearts. It is simply a result of what was taught to them. Today's generation has broken the mould by innately desiring a more balanced advancement, the successful interweaving of mind and heart wisdom, diverse perspectives, and global awareness.

One-sided viewpoints established by cultural traditions or parental limitations that may have grounded past societies lead to disconnect and negation with today's children. They crave interdependence, independence, and universal connections that enhance life. From the knowledge of the past, and the current insight of the modern day world, children are able to observe the "seeding" of people and experiences, and how they conform to ideals that can add to what individuals need to progress.

Today's children require deeply engaging, higher consciousness experiences that provide effective, nurturing, mindful opportunities that are beneficial for all people. The attention to life challenges is precisely what builds character and a strong sense of self that helps today's generation navigate successfully in a global world. The muscle behind children's ways of thinking has to do with a collaboration of multidimensional perspectives and voices that build a personal sense of the world. Parents who *Teach and Engage* recognize their responsibility in affirming the value in all elements of life experiences.

Joyful existence happens when people experience life lessons that are beneficial to personal growth. Learning through engaging entails fresh, multifaceted experiences, and new perspectives, which combine intuition, innovation, and discovery. People tread farther than ever-imagined possible when they steer toward their dreams and passions in a free and fluid mind-set. Those who aspire to reach fulfillment, which encompasses happiness but, is more satisfying and empowering, need to have trust in an unlimited potential and an acceptance of what is.

Any individual journeying toward fulfillment or wisdom is actually discovering who they are while focusing on their personal goals and intention. The more people strive joyfully and authentically, the more they elevate feelings and beliefs of who they can become – the closer the get to understanding their potential wisdom. A conscious depth of awareness creates a solid foundation that advances greater life opportunities. The greater one's awareness, the clearer his or her own wisdom becomes. An acceptance of what is along with trust in the fact that each individual has the power within them to make the best choices support individuals in reaching true wisdom. See diagram below.

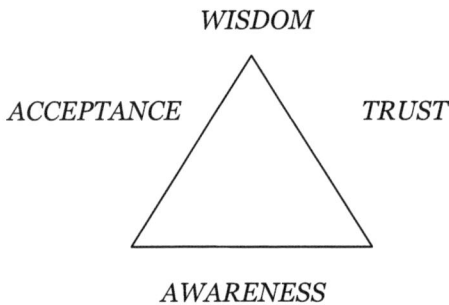

WISDOM

ACCEPTANCE   *TRUST*

AWARENESS

At this time in history, it is my belief that we are on a path of conscious learning and teaching of each other. Essentially, parents are the spheres of influence for their children. They help children build upon their awareness. That is why they need to remain open to the magnitude of this unique generation of children by teaching them loving, optimistic, meaningful life lessons. This is the energy behind raising standards and creating relevant learning in today's world. People nowadays have the opportunity to knowingly invest time to *Teach and Engage* children so to inspire, elevate expectations, and ultimately build bridges of self-worth among humanity. Choosing confidence over risk will be the path toward freedom for modern day parents.

Trusting in the overall philosophy of *Wing It* allows parents to help their children become positive life contributors. The Teach and Engage strategy embraces the concept of loving children unconditionally and helping them feel safe as they expand in love and wisdom. It is about gaining insight to understand children and respecting their presence graciously. To *Teach and Engage* confidently as individuals discover personal paths helps them resolve issues and casts hopefulness as they make advancements in their lives. Parents need to love them madly as they discover their potential. Children will do well when the people who surround them accept them and value their contributions. The influence from the circumstances children are exposed to will propel them further than imagined.

Conclusion

⚶

THE LAUNCH

The future belongs to those who believe in the beauty of their dreams. - Eleanor Roosevelt

The commitment to parenting is a precious opportunity to grow into a better person, immensely influence another person's life, and to launch children and yourself to becoming personally fulfilled. No matter what you've heard, there is no one "right" way to parent. Intention is what matters most, and at no other point in time have families been so beautifully diverse yet remain unyielding with the united intention to be better parents and raise children successfully in today's world. This open purpose promotes parenting to be ever changing, and chalk full of potential for families to grow significantly.

Life is full of challenges disguised in many ways, but learning from these opportunities is all part of each person's journey. Parents of today have one thing in common: they know better and want to be better parents. Fortunately, with all the advancements of this century, they have the chance to do just that on their own terms, at their own pace, and growing their own set of beliefs and practices that compliment their families and aspirations.

In today's world with this highly inspired generation of children come individual styles and dynamic family structures. The assortment of families, preferences, abilities, and ambitions propels cooperation that can catapult individuals to greatness. As people develop stronger ideals and practices they naturally shed false ideas and limiting mindsets. People who practice parenting that reflects genuine understanding and acceptance teach children how to honor who they are and the significance they bring to this world. That is how actual success is initiated. Success is in the process, not just the end result.

Everyday, moment-to-moment living that is guided by intuition and creativity renews personal achievement and brings about success. In today's world it presents itself as a back-to-basics type of parenting that is also complementary to modern life. The practices resonate with people who yearn for a distinction from the false notion that others may hold about the difficulty of living with children and are ready to launch new paradigms for parenting. Parents make parenthood as hard as they want it. But, it certainly doesn't have to be that way. The *Wing It* prescription is based on parents knowing better and doing better, not working harder. More over, this leads individuals to arrive at their personal goals a heck of a lot easier and a family life that is organically more fluid and fun.

Parents today are able to progress forward with new choices, new perspectives, and new beliefs. They have the power to make tremendous change when they put forth the necessary commitment, cooperation, and vision using the essential principles in this book as modern day parents. This past decade has bombarded parents with radical approaches to raising children instead of supporting the time-honored wisdom found within each human being. Every single person has the choice to make parenthood easy or hard.

Life allows so many variables on how individuals can parent successfully. Despite widespread skepticism and negativity in the world, parents have the most worthwhile and flexible paths to raise children today. It is quite a departure from how previous generations were raised and taught. Parenting does not need to include shame, anger, fear, judgment, embarrassment, or stress. Rather, individuals can take back their rights to release false notions that limit them and look toward empowering themselves as freethinking, progressive parents.

Advancements in today's generation may cause some confusion and trepidation for parents who are trying to raise well-balanced, successful children. We live in a diverse, fast-paced, often times unstable world where parents have the grand task of raising smart, independent, and responsible people. Those who design cooperative dynamics and environments that are aligned with universal wisdom and personal ideas will launch children to success with more simplicity.

To avoid the pressures of external ideals, and become confident parents is something that happens over time and with a commitment to the greater good of your self, your family, and the world. It is also very doable. Once there is awareness and a strong intent to change, parents are able to get back into the driver's seat and launch their children and families toward independent success.

The combined formula presented throughout this book in part one: *Root It* and part two: *Wing It* suggests that contemporary parents can be practical yet soulful as they utilize creative initiatives to raise today's children. Overall, there exists balance for those parents who provide fertile space that fosters roots and wings. In this case, balance doesn't mean standing still ever without falling over. Rather a solution of remaining flexible and embracing the pushes and pulls of life. People will evolve to their best selves with this balance. It is each individual's personal attitude that contributes to the significant moves toward success.

Wing It practices can inspire individuals to be the best people that they were born to be, and the best parents they wish to be. It's a new way of thinking for a brand new generation that is ready for an uplifting shift that brings more awareness and innovation to life experiences. Today's children and parents have the capacity and potential to be monumental innovators, thinkers, and doers.

The world provides a plethora of divergent voices that become exaggerated even more so when venturing into parenting. The greatest conflict occurs when parents disregard their internal wisdom and allow themselves to be bombarded with loud, unnecessary criticisms and expectations that hinder unique paths of possibilities. Society's busyness, materialism, and need for instant gratification has often made people lose the capacity to live joyously.

Wing It can be used as a guide to develop an all-embracing voice that propels perfect paths for parenting, and permeates lives with meaningful connections and experiences. An overarching insight of self-expression in parenting allows people to grow. To value and follow personal convictions are critical in raising 21st century children. Committing to the importance of wellness and social-emotional-spiritual growth within families helps individuals create new visions for growing children during this pivotal time of change. Life is continuous. So, it allows people to collect meaning as they build on their experiences and follow personal architectures that help them accomplish just that.

Change starts within each individual. Even one application of a suggestion illustrated in *Wing It* can generate ripples that awaken personal potential and empowerment. The ideas shared encourage building a foundation first in order to sprout to a higher realm by trusting more, listening deeper, and looking within to make changes that foster self-confidence and a respect for diverse purposes.

The practice of honoring a natural sense of wonder while engaging meaningfully with today's children has the power to make enormous changes within this generation. As people shed insecurities and negative layers that obstruct evolution, they will be able to sense new possibilities and gain more wisdom. Now is the time to recreate belief systems and dream bigger dreams so children in today's world can be the visionaries this world needs. A change in beliefs changes the conversation and that creates emerging possibilities that exemplify living wholly and creatively with children while sustaining the integrity of each individual.

The *Wing It* movement is about changing individual mindsets and approaching parenting in a freeing confident manner in order to allow individual greatness to emerge. This generation of children already recognizes the importance of honoring their limitless possibilities in a more harmonious way than previous groups. They figure stuff out before parents and schools even begin to teach them. That alone can be very intimidating for today's parents. But, at the same token, it becomes a wonderful opportunity for relationships between parents and children to reach deepened levels of understanding. Individuals who ignore negative influences, make choices using intuition, and parent with ease can move closer to applying the *Wing It* formula to see positive change in their lives.

We are at the dawn of a new day in parenting, a radically different scope of expectations and acceptance where parents can respectfully disregard the parenting myths of perfection, and notice the best in themselves and their children. People who believe in and practice *Wing It* concepts become self-empowered because they gain an expansion in consciousness that honors their individuality.

Problems and conflicts arise when people deny their own truths. That is why there exists such divisiveness when discussing which approach is best. When people go against the natural order to life resistance appears, fears form, and alarming viewpoints expand. All these components delay happiness. Every person has the potential to raise excellent children by following what they know to be true for themselves and their children.

Parents who walk progressively in reflection and remain open to changing patterns in situations that are not working for them can find their truth. Enlightened moments often come through the soft voice of intuition when people are too tired or frustrated to keep doing what they think is best. It happens with me all the time.

After letting go, I mean really letting go, of any fear-based premonitions about who my children would or would not grow up to be, I became a better parent. The moment I surrendered my concerns and worries about the unknown hardships they were doomed to experience if they did not change this personality trait or that attitude led to an internal release and shift that amended my individual relationships with my children and strengthened our resolve.

Children are intuitive. They "get" life and are the greatest teachers of life. With the simplest and purest ideas and questions they embody wisdom beyond their years. Parents who can resist urges to focus on potential signs of greatness, or lack thereof, gain easier insight and recognize the gifts they are here to share. Remaining attentive to individual preferences and likes are all part of the journey of life. Those who respond to their child's talent in a timely and curious manner spark opportunities that will arouse their passion.

Parents must simply manage and cultivate a child's interest without imposing an authoritative mandate of mastery. Success in parenting should be measured by the incredible moments of remaining present experienced throughout the organic journey of life, not by a forced execution of a check-off list that society says parents must accomplish. It is not about simply showing up to public events to make it look good from the outside, but really being aware during those enlightened moments with children as they discover life.

We often hear parents bragging about where their children go to college, or what profession they hold. Well, what does it cost to a child's spirit to get them there? More often than not, in life there are all too often struggles, frustrations, or mandatory steps made by caregivers in an effort to gain labels. Unfortunately, society measures success by accomplishments in schools that educate today's children in dated, homogeneous, strenuous systems.

It reminds me of when a saw a father moan and groan as he fixed his son's bicycle. He complained the whole time and expected the child to be overjoyed when he finished. That child felt the negative energy as he fixed it, and felt uneasy with the process. Had his father repaired the bicycle with ease and joy he would have shown authentic gratitude when it was given to him instead of guilt or shame. When something is done with love, it is understood and appreciated naturally by a child who feels valued. Just like the homemade cookies baked with love. They simply taste better. The fun part is the journey, the physical, emotional, and spiritual expenditure toward a fulfilling moment. More importantly, raising today's children is about the interaction shared in just being together. As you parent, be cautious of your intent and energy displayed.

Parents who design approaches that feel right are supported and naturally rid their lives of chaos, relish in the delightfulness of living with children, and set themselves up for future success. This is an opportunity to give a voice to the truth, make peace with the past and heal, and formulate an agreement that is complimentary to your personality and potential.

There exists a collaborative spirit in the current world of progressive parenting – an appreciation for individuality. Most parents know there is an easier way and want to change but don't know where to begin. Begin here. The nature in building independent practices is part of the natural order of this new generation and the evolution of spirit-conscious human beings. Like never before, parents are being challenged by the need to always be prepared for the next step and follow through with raising bright, well-rounded, responsible, culturally astute children. Using the *Wing It* strategies helps parents accomplish just that, a successful approach in honoring themselves and launching their children to their potential.

In this complex world, people generate their own restrictions in life and must work hard to detach themselves from being controlled by scripts written in the past that won't work in today's times. When individuals change, life adapts. The joy of winging it reap rewards that increase personal resiliency to outside critics along with gaining real consideration for individual insight that creates better lives.

Exponentially building strong foundations and trusting in themselves will thrust people to design relevant roles and experiences that are beneficial for them, and help individuals choose confidence over fear. Life confronts people with issues and situations that they need for advancement. Winging it helps people disengage from unconstructive mindsets and change any encumbered circumstances. Parents can then begin exploring what it is they do want and the possibilities of reconstructing an amazing life. It is time for parents to form a new vision and walk in their wisdom to create new paths for their well-being and happiness.

The truth of the matter is that it takes a whole lot of energy, patience, open-mindedness, and humor to master the art of parenting well. The willingness to care for oneself first so that individuals are able to share their best in all relationships is totally attainable. There are few experiences on earth that will stretch your spirit more than parenthood. Whether someone is raising one, three, or ten children, if they have the guts to free themselves from irrelevant expectations and judgments, they can make staggering strides towards becoming their best selves. Parents who have independent visions can be like the wild flowers that break through the cracks, authentically growing without needing too much fussing over or attention. These sprouts continuously grow towards the point of light with faith and a purpose to expand.

Parenthood is about valuing our worth and our role, as we do the moment we become endowed with the miraculous task of becoming parents. The parenting journey should be more of a creative progression and not a reactive response to controlling the entanglement of moments presented, to nurture individual's aspirations rather than fight to survive.

As parents, it is our job to not only provide the light for our children but also, to find out the point of entrance into our purpose and ride the wave of enlightenment. The ripple effects of tapping into the soul of purpose and teaching children to do the same is a continual task that works in full partnership with the world at large if done authentically. Global experiences and new perspectives help people recognize the vastness of possibilities and individual capacity to learn physically, spiritually, emotionally, intellectually and symbolically. Moving through life motivated by the Wing It philosophy will diffuse the complexities of our time.

The term "Namaste" has become a more and more popular salutation recently. Having a literal translation in Sanskrit of "I bow to you" it is an endearing phrase that tells people they are valued. It is spoken with the belief that there exists a divine spark within each of us and when we are open to receiving love we can connect on a soul-to-soul level, ridding our lives with the nonsensical minutia. Just as I was finishing up writing this book I came to a realization that "Namaste", phonetically translated in Greek, means a mutual hope of "let us be." A common phrase heard by two or more Greeks wishing each other well is "Namaste Kala" meaning "let us all be well." These two simple ideas of "I bow to you" and "let us be" sum up the nuance behind *Wing It*. If we respect one another, see each other's beauty, and live from the heart our spirits will blossom and the world will be well.

I wish you well and that *Wing It* will provide you, the reader, an opportunity to share prosperity, voice of reason, and a common vision of optimism for raising children in today's world. When feeling like you are swimming against the current of life renew your sense of wisdom by referencing part one of this book that combines ideas that set an anchor for solid foundations that help house the essential parts of living happily with children.

The strategies of *Wing It* can surely be practiced independent of each other but become more powerful when used in a united way. As you build new perspectives and use intuition to cultivate nurturing environments for your children, allow time and space for your new self to take root and expand beyond your wildest ambitions. Winging it is about happier, less complicated, and more fulfilling experiences throughout the course of parenthood, not just one destination to be reached. It is an inspired process, a launching of our best selves and the best within our children. As you try to master parenthood, remember that anything is possible. It just takes time to disconnect from the things you've been taught that hinder happiness and a reconnection with limitless optimism to be your best self in this lifetime. Putting into practice the formula presented in this book will help you make life with children easier and help you create magnificent life experiences. Allow *Wing It* to work for you.

The end

WING IT™
6 Simple Steps to Succeed as a Modern Day Parent

By Anastasia Gavalas

Welcome Children Into the Process

Intuit Your Success

Navigate their Life-Education

Get Real Simple

Inspire Independence

Teach and Engage

Anastasia Gavalas, *MS, SDA* is a family life teacher, national parenting contributor, and mother of five who believes that parenting doesn't have to be the hardest job on earth. She understands that in today's world families have a lot going on, and finding the best approach isn't in a one-size-fits-all solution. Life with children is made less complicated and easier with the innovative ways she shares in *Wing It*. This book was born out of her work with families and the belief that every person has the potential to create fulfilling experiences as they progress in parenthood and in life.

To connect with Anastasia visit her website

www.anastasiagavalas.com

email: Anastasia@anastasiagavalas.com

Like her page:

www.facebook.com/AnastasiaGavalasFanpage

Follow her on Twitter: @anastasia1970